Cambridge Elements ≡

Elements in Philosophy of Law
edited by
George Pavlakos
University of Glasgow
Gerald J. Postema
University of North Carolina at Chapel Hill
Kenneth M. Ehrenberg
University of Surrey
Sally Zhu
University of Sheffield

DIGNITY AND RIGHTS

Ariel Zylberman
University at Albany
State University of New York

CAMBRIDGE
UNIVERSITY PRESS

Shaftesbury Road, Cambridge CB2 8EA, United Kingdom

One Liberty Plaza, 20th Floor, New York, NY 10006, USA

477 Williamstown Road, Port Melbourne, VIC 3207, Australia

314–321, 3rd Floor, Plot 3, Splendor Forum, Jasola District Centre,
New Delhi – 110025, India

103 Penang Road, #05–06/07, Visioncrest Commercial, Singapore 238467

Cambridge University Press is part of Cambridge University Press & Assessment,
a department of the University of Cambridge.

We share the University's mission to contribute to society through the pursuit
of education, learning and research at the highest international levels of excellence.

www.cambridge.org
Information on this title: www.cambridge.org/9781009565134

DOI: 10.1017/9781009238601

First published 2025

A catalogue record for this publication is available from the British Library

ISBN 978-1-009-56513-4 Hardback
ISBN 978-1-009-23857-1 Paperback
ISSN 2631-5815 (online)
ISSN 2631-5807 (print)

Cambridge University Press & Assessment has no responsibility for the persistence
or accuracy of URLs for external or third-party internet websites referred to in this
publication and does not guarantee that any content on such websites is, or will
remain, accurate or appropriate.

Dignity and Rights

Elements in Philosophy of Law

DOI: 10.1017/9781009238601
First published online: January 2025

Ariel Zylberman
University at Albany
State University of New York

Author for correspondence: Ariel Zylberman, azylberman@albany.edu

Abstract: Dignity and rights are pervasive ideas. But how exactly should we understand them? Although philosophical theories of dignity and of rights typically proceed independently of each other, this Element treats them together. One advantage of doing so is that we can see a deeper unity underlying the familiar difficulties of standard accounts of dignity and rights (Sections 1 and 2). A second advantage is that understanding how many of the difficulties stem from the reductivist structure of the standard accounts lets us envisage a nonreductivist alternative. Drawing from the metaphysics of kinds and dispositions and from social ontology shows that dignity and rights are fundamental and interdependent normative properties. As pre-conventional properties (Section 3), dignity and rights mark a distinct type of value and function dispositionally, directed to actualization through recognition by others. As social properties (Section 4), they specify the normative status and entitlements constitutive of social kinds.

Keywords: dignity, rights, relational norms, ethics, philosophy of law

ISBNs: 9781009565134 (HB), 9781009238571 (PB), 9781009238601 (OC)
ISSNs: 2631-5815 (online), 2631-5807 (print)

Contents

Introduction   1

1 Dignity: Between Naturalism and Conventionalism   4

2 Rights: Between Naturalism and Conventionalism   18

3 Natural Rights: A Kind-Dispositional Model   36

4 Conventional Rights: A Kind-Dispositional Model   59

   References   77

Introduction

"Respect for persons (this is an intriguing idea) may simply be respect for their rights, so that there cannot be the one without the other," said philosopher Joel Feinberg once (Feinberg 1970: 252). This Element is an exploration of Feinberg's intriguing idea.

The idea that the dignity of persons and their rights depend on each other might be intriguing to the philosopher, but can seem commonsensical when we're not doing philosophy.

As the horrors of the Holocaust seared themselves in German self-consciousness, the German Basic Law of 1949 proclaimed that "the dignity of persons is inviolable" and that the "German people therefore acknowledge inviolable and inalienable human rights as the basis of every community, of peace and justice in the world."[1] Roughly at the same time, the Universal Declaration of Human Rights began with a recognition of the "inherent dignity ... of all the members of the human family," quickly adding that all "human beings are born free and equal in dignity and rights." Both of these foundational postwar legal documents appear to uphold Feinberg's intriguing idea: respect for the dignity of persons is conceptually tied to respect for their basic rights.

Feinberg's intriguing idea is not confined to legal documents from the 1940s. Rather, it can seem almost omnipresent. We can't help but reach for the language of the dignity of persons and their rights when we face the deep injustices of our time. Here are just two examples.

In his historic closing argument in the 1985 trial against the junta leaders of Argentina who had overseen the rape, torture, murder, and disappearances of thousands, Julio Strassera reached for the language of dignity and rights. No matter how fine your end might seem to you, Strassera argued, an attack on the inviolable dignity of the human person and their rights can never be justified.[2]

---

[1] Die Grundrechte Art 1 (1) Die Würde des Menschen ist unantastbar. Sie zu achten und zu schützen ist Verpflichtung aller staatlichen Gewalt. (2) Das Deutsche Volk bekennt sich darum zu unverletzlichen und unveräußerlichen Menschenrechten als Grundlage jeder menschlichen Gemeinschaft, des Friedens und der Gerechtigkeit in der Welt ((1)Human dignity shall be inviolable. To respect and protect it shall be the duty of all state authority. (2) The German people therefore acknowledge inviolable and inalienable human rights as the basis of every community, of peace and of justice in the world).

[2] "Si bien a veces pueden aplicarse medidas especiales para garantizar la seguridad de las personas, ellas nunca jamás justifican un ataque a la dignidad inviolable de la persona humana y a los derechos que protegen su dignidad. Si cierta ideología y ciertas formas de interpretar la legítima preocupación por la seguridad nacional dieran como resultado el subyugar el Estado, al hombre y sus derechos y dignidad, ellas cesarían en la misma medida de ser humanas" ("Even if sometimes special measures may be taken to guarantee the security of persons, such measures never justify an attack on the inviolable dignity of the human person and on the rights that protect such dignity. If some ideology and some forms of interpreting the rightful concern for national

American civil rights advocate and legal scholar Michelle Alexander methodically argues that the racial caste system that characterized antebellum America did not entirely disappear but transformed: once through the Jim Crow socio-legal structure, then in the civil rights era through the socio-legal structure of mass incarceration. Alexander concludes that the drug war is the new Jim Crow and ends with a positive vision where "all human beings of all races are treated with dignity, and have the right to food, shelter, health care, education, and security" (Alexander 2010: 246).

Although the German Basic Law, the UN Declaration, Julio Strassera, and Michelle Alexander all endorse the idea that dignity, respect, and rights are intimately connected, that's not an idea you'd find among philosophers. The now vast literatures on the nature of dignity and rights, with notable exceptions, appear as distinct, isolated silos. Leading philosophical analyses of the concept of dignity often make no reference to the concept of a right, while leading philosophical analyses of the concept of rights typically make no reference to the concept of dignity. If these philosophical theories are correct, not only is Feinberg's intriguing idea not self-evident; it's not even true.

How can an idea seem both deep and trivially true but also false?

To start thinking through this puzzle, in this Element I'll take you through some of the leading philosophical accounts of dignity and of rights. And since the literature on these topics is vast, I'll focus exclusively on the formal question of the nature of dignity and rights (what is dignity? What are rights?) setting aside equally important but more substantive questions (who exactly has dignity? What specific requirements does dignity generate? Who exactly has rights? What rights do we have?). But as I hope to show you, already at the abstract formal level, there is a deep philosophical disagreement.

Section 1 begins with dignity. One of the fundamental questions about dignity is whether dignity is pre-conventional. On the one hand, what I'll call "naturalist" views argue that dignity is best understood as an invulnerable normative property possessed by individuals in isolation, in virtue of their nature. On the other hand, what I'll call "conventionalist" views argue that dignity is an extrinsic and relational normative property. However, both analyses face serious difficulties meeting reasonable explanatory demands: naturalist accounts struggle to explain why the recognition of dignity matters in the way it seems to; conventionalist accounts struggle to explain why dignity seemingly binds us independently of conventional social facts.

---

security resulted in subordinating the state, man, and his rights and dignity, they would to that extent cease being human.") (Strassera 2024).

Section 2 turns to the concept of rights and explores a loosely parallel debate. What many contemporary philosophers take to be "the" central debate in rights theory is whether the paradigmatic role of rights is to protect interests or to safeguard choices. Though Interest and Will theories (as they are now known) can accommodate conventional rights, they are not committed to the thesis that rights are necessarily conventional. By contrast, a long philosophical tradition including at least Thomas Hobbes, Jeremy Bentham, and T.H. Green does uphold the conventionalist thesis that, necessarily, rights are conventional. Bentham articulated the idea colorfully:

> Right, the substantive right, is the child of law: from real laws come real rights; but from imaginary laws, from laws of nature, fancied and invented by poets, rhetoricians, and dealers in moral and intellectual poisons, come imaginary rights, a bastard brood of monsters, "gorgons and chimaeras dire." (1987: 46)

Hyperbole aside, Bentham's central point is powerful: real rights require actual social recognition. More recently, Rex Martin (1993) and Derrick Darby (2009) have defended versions of the conventionalist core in Bentham's thought. With the contrast in view, I explain briefly why these familiar accounts seem to face stubborn difficulties.

By the end of Section 2, we'll face a fork on the road.

On the one hand, you could try to refine one of the familiar views, showing that standard objections can be sidestepped. Nothing I say in this Element is meant to show that this is not a worthwhile task. Indeed, my hope is that by connecting conceptual resources from the typically isolated silos of the theories of rights and dignity, further theoretical refinement might be gained.

On the other hand, you could try to take seriously Feinberg's intriguing idea and seek an alternative. That's what I begin to do in Sections 3 and 4.

Drawing from metaphilosophy, I question the prevailing assumption that a good philosophical explanation should provide a *reductivist analysis*. However, reductive analyses typically face a dilemma. Either they fail to offer noncircular *sufficient* conditions (i.e., the explanans isn't sufficient to explain the explanandum), or they fail to offer *noncircular* sufficient conditions (the explanans is sufficient but only by presupposing the explanandum). A neglected but promising way to avoid the dilemma is to abandon altogether the model of reductive analysis and to replace it, perhaps, with what P.F. Strawson called the model of "holistic elucidation" (1992). The model explains by elucidating the function a concept plays in a network. In particular, the model seeks to find concepts that play a distinctive role: concepts that are irreducible not because they can't be *decomposed* further, but because they are *fundamental* – relative to some relevant domain. And they are fundamental because eliminating them would entail eliminating a whole host of other concepts that depend on them.

Having shifted to a non-reductivist model of explanation, I then draw from a *metaphysics* of kinds and dispositions. Many contemporary moral and political philosophers seek scrupulously to disengage from any robust metaphysical commitments. By contrast, I believe that a metaphysics of kinds and dispositions is key to understand the nature of dignity and rights. More specifically, I'll begin to explore a "Kind-Dispositional" view.

Section 3 develops the following analogy. Just as non-normative dispositions exist prior to manifestation but are actualized or made real through manifestation (e.g., the solubility of water is manifested only when salt or sugar interacts with water), so too natural dignity and rights exist prior to recognition but are actualized or completed through interpersonal relations of recognition. As natural categories, the function of dignity is to characterize a distinctive type of value, one that is logically connected to "deontic" properties of respect. But since such properties of respect correlate with claim-rights, dignity and rights are not just fundamental categories, they are also essentially interdependent.

Section 4 develops the model for social kinds. The basic idea is that dignity and rights play the function of constituting the normative status and normative entitlements essential to specific social kinds, such as being a citizen, a government official, an employee, or a parent.

In the end, my aim is not to convince you that a non-reductivist, Kind-Dispositional model is true. After all, I can only sketch the model here. Instead, my aim is twofold. First, by exploring a neglected parallel in philosophical accounts of dignity and rights, I hope I can make available resources for further refinement of the familiar theories. And since most familiar theories are reductivist, my second aim is to begin opening up space for what a non-reductivist explanation might look like. A key advantage of such an explanation, I argue, is that it can bypass the dilemma affecting reductivist models in moral, legal, and political philosophy. A second advantage is that the model invites you to think of dignity and rights as much more dynamic, active, and relational properties than the standard views allow. Thus, we might come to understand why dignity and rights are indeed the fundamental and essentially interdependent categories of practical thought we take them to be when we're not doing philosophy.

1 Dignity: Between Naturalism and Conventionalism

In this section I turn to the topic of dignity and examine the two most important types of philosophical accounts, one naturalist, the other conventionalist. In doing so, I'll set aside substantive questions about the scope and extension of the concept of dignity. I begin by explaining at least two conditions that a good analysis of dignity should meet: it should explain the distinct *normativity* of dignity – how it correlates with overriding duties of respect – and the *significance* of recognition – why misrecognition of dignity matters. I'll argue that though naturalist and conventionalist accounts have important insights, they struggle to accommodate both conditions. What's more, both accounts struggle to explain the relational structure of dignity, that is, how dignity is not just a value to be promoted or even an impersonal norm to be observed, but a personal entitlement to be respected. Highlighting the significance of entitlements to the notion of dignity will help us transition to the topic of rights in the next section.

1.1 Dignity: Some Preliminaries

Let's begin by introducing the notion of dignity and some preliminary conditions a satisfactory account of dignity should either meet or explain away.

First, let's distinguish the formal question of the nature of dignity from the substantive question of who exactly has dignity and why. The formal question is about what kind of normative property dignity is supposed to be. The substantive question is about scope (who exactly has dignity?) and ground (in virtue of what specific properties does a being have dignity?).

In this Element I'll focus exclusively on the formal type of question for two reasons. For one thing, there is a sense in which the formal question is logically prior. For instance, if it turns out that the notion of a natural right is nonsense upon stilts, as Jeremy Bentham once quipped, then it makes no sense to try to figure out what specific natural rights we have or who has them. Similarly, if it turned out that neither naturalist nor conventionalist views of dignity made much sense, it would make little sense to try to figure out who should count as a bearer of dignity. For another, sheer reasons of space suggest against tackling both inquiries at once. Besides, focusing on the formal question will let us explore an important connection between formal questions about dignity and rights.

Let's refine the formal question further, given that the term "dignity" is used in many ways. As Jeremy Waldron remarks, there's a distinction between a kind of dignity that is *achieved* – gained or lost through one's actions – from a kind of dignity that is *inherent*.[3] For instance, when people speak of "dying with dignity" or of the dignity that is achieved by acting virtuously or morally,

---

[3] Waldron (2012: 58–9). See also Gilabert (2015: 199) and (2019). As we'll see next, conventionalist accounts of dignity make some trouble for this distinction.

they have in mind a property that is achieved or lost. By contrast, when the preambles to the International Covenants on human rights speak of rights "derived from the inherent dignity of the human person," they are not referring to rights that are gained or lost through the good actions of individuals. Rather, the idea is that this kind of dignity is not achieved, but is a necessary, inherent property of individuals. Let's call inherent dignity *fundamental* and achieved dignity *derivative*.[4]

As we'll see next, the connection between fundamental and derivative dignity is complicated. But for now, the distinction helps to sharpen our formal question: how should the idea of fundamental dignity be understood and justified?

A good philosophical answer to this question, it seems, should meet at least two important desiderata.[5]

Call the first the Deontic Normativity Condition:

> *Deontic Normativity Condition*: Fundamental dignity necessarily entails a stringent duty of respect.

Dignity doesn't simply correlate with normative reasons understood as considerations in favor of a given course of action. For instance, the fact that I have a soft spot for good espressos is a consideration in favor of preferring this espresso here over the fast-food coffee over there. By contrast, dignity has what we may call "deontic structure," entailing a stringent obligation or duty of respect.[6] Unlike my preference for coffee – which does not necessarily entail obligations or stringent duties – your dignity appears to conceptually implicate a distinct kind of reason for me, one that typically overrides (or silences, preempts, or excludes) competing considerations. If I don't happen to like coffee, then I lack reasons to have any coffee at all. By contrast, your dignity

---

[4] I prefer "fundamental" to "human" dignity in order to leave open the substantive question of whether some nonhuman animals have fundamental dignity.

[5] Zylberman (2016a). However, the formulation here is slightly different. The philosophical literature on dignity is now too vast to do it full justice in this short Element. As a result, I will inevitably leave out important contributions and have to pick only some representative views. For recent important books on the topic, see Rosen (2012), Waldron (2012), Gilabert (2019), Killmister (2020), and Bird (2021). For important collections, see McCrudden (2014) and Düwell et al. (2015). For articulations of what I'm calling the normativity condition, see Christiano (2008), Green (2010), Waldron (2012), Düwell et al. (2015), Gilabert (2019), and Killmister (2020). What I'll call the recognition condition is emphasized by Killmister (2017: 2064–5) as the vulnerability condition and by Bird (2021).

[6] See Wallace (2013, 2019). For discussion of this deontic aspect of dignity see Christiano (2008), Düwell et al. (2015: 27), and Gilabert (2019: 124). To clarify: the notion of entailment here is conceptual rather than substantive or explanatory. The idea is simply that fundamental dignity conceptually correlates with a robust duty of respect, not necessarily that dignity generates or explains a duty of respect – though the latter may also be true. Thanks to an anonymous referee for pressing me to clarify.

still binds me to respect you regardless of how I happen to feel or what I happen to like.

The opening lines of the German Basic Law seem to express the Deontic Normativity condition when they describe fundamental dignity as "inviolable" (*unantastbar*). The inviolability of dignity is not meant to express merely a high degree of value (like me having a stronger preference for espressos over commercial drip coffee) but a different kind of consideration, one that sets an overriding obligation of respect. After all, in German the term *unantastbar* connotes not just inviolable but also "sacrosanct."

It seems, then, that a philosophical analysis of fundamental dignity should explain how dignity differs from other values or reasons and necessarily entails a stringent duty of respect.

At the same time, a philosophical analysis needs to explain why dignity and the correlative duty of respect matter in the distinctive way they do. Why do the misrecognition and violation of dignity matter? Call this the Recognition Condition.

> *Recognition Condition*: The misrecognition and violation of fundamental dignity matters deeply.

A good analysis of dignity should explain, then, why dignity can seem so vulnerable to damage and misrecognition (Killmister 2017: 2064–5) and how it's importantly at risk when some agents violate their duty to respect the dignity of others (Bird 2021: 78). For instance, when Strassera condemned the military junta for the torture and rape of political prisoners, he was condemning how such acts seriously damaged the dignity of victims. When Alexander condemns the relegation to second-class moral status of Black individuals and the accompanying loss of fundamental rights, she too condemns the serious misrecognition of and damage to the dignity of Black individuals. Strassera and Alexander, as I read them, are giving voice to the Recognition Condition.

Having sharpened our formal question about fundamental dignity, I think philosophical answers to this question can be grouped into roughly *naturalist* and *conventionalist* accounts. Let's examine how they seek to meet the normativity and recognition conditions.

1.2 Dignity Naturalism

After explaining some core conceptual commitments of Dignity Naturalism, I'll argue that Dignity Naturalism can fare well with the Normativity Condition, but struggles with the Recognition condition.

Here's a rough, preliminary formulation of the view:[7]

> **Dignity Naturalism**. Dignity is the inherent, non-relational, and non-instrumental value of an agent.

First, a clarification of the term "naturalism." By this term I don't mean a property that is available to the hard empirical sciences, such as physics or chemistry, but rather a property whose existence is not dependent on specific conventions or practices.

Inherent properties contrast with acquired ones. Your dignity is inherent in the sense that you possess it regardless of specific actions or circumstantial contingencies qualifying you, say, as an Australian or a Muslim.

Non-relational properties contrast with relational ones. Dignity would be non-relational in the sense that you possess it regardless of any specific relations you may bear to others – and even in the absence of all others.

Non-instrumental values contrast with instrumental values, that is, things that are valued merely as means for the promotion of other values. Dignity is a non-instrumental value in the sense that your dignity is valuable in itself rather than as a means for the production of some further value, such as the production of happiness or compliance with tradition.

The final term in the formulation is "agent." I should emphasize that the formula does not necessarily restrict agency to the chief topic of philosophers of action, namely, *intentional* agency. On the contrary, Dignity Naturalism could be specified with maximally wide scope – say, a biocentric view that assigns dignity to all living beings – medium scope – say, only to sentient beings – or with much narrower scope – say, only to rational beings.

Just as Dignity Naturalism leaves open the question of scope, for the same reason it leaves open the substantive question of what properties, exactly, make it the case that you have dignity. This means that a variety of philosophical traditions fit within the wide umbrella of Dignity Naturalism.

For (many) Kantians, your dignity consists in your rational nature as an *end in itself* (Korsgaard 1996; Wood 1999; Formosa and Mackenzie 2014; Formosa 2017; Gilabert 2019). For (many) Catholics, your dignity consists in your having been created in the image of God (Rosen 2012: 148). For (many) neo-Aristotelians, your dignity consists in the value of your basic capabilities (Nussbaum 2007; Nussbaum 2008). Some teleological philosophers argue that your dignity consists in the basic good of human nature (Griffin 2008; Tasioulas 2013: 305). Although these are competing accounts of what specific properties are necessary and sufficient for a being to *possess* dignity, all these

---

[7] See Gilabert (2019: 124).

accounts share a more general and abstract commitment to Dignity Naturalism. Our focus is not on the specifications of the proposal, but the proposal itself.

So ask: is Dignity Naturalism true? Should dignity be understood as an inherent, non-instrumental, and non-relational value?

An initial advantage of Dignity Naturalism is that it seems well placed to meet the normativity condition. If dignity is an inherent property, it's not a normative property that can be lost. Further, if dignity is a non-instrumental value, then we can begin to see why dignity might entail particularly stringent duties. As Allen Wood puts the point in a loosely Kantian way, "the incomparable worth of the human being means that human dignity can never rationally be sacrificed or traded away for anything at all, not even for something else having dignity" (Wood 1999: 49). The idea, then, is that once we capture the inherent and non-instrumental value that constitutes dignity, the stringent duty of respect comes, as it were, for free: it's packed into the concept of fundamental dignity. If so, Dignity Naturalism would meet the Normativity Condition with ease.

Nevertheless, it is worth pausing here to reflect on whether Dignity Naturalism, as formulated, can indeed explain how fundamental dignity entails a stringent duty of respect. The point is subtle and technical, but important. There is reason to suspect that the notion of value as such need not entail the duties of respect characteristic of dignity.

To see this point, consider other things that might instantiate a non-instrumental value. When reflecting on the nature of value, Brazilian philosopher Miguel Reale once asked that we try to compare the value of Bernini's David with Michelangelo's David. Reale's argument is that you can't compare these and establish objectively which is, say, "more beautiful." And that's an argument to the conclusion that "the idea of numeration or quantification is completely alien to the valuative or axiological element" (Reale 2004: 207). Suppose, then, that Reale is right: Bernini and Michelangelo's works of art possess non-instrumental and non-comparative value. But does it follow that such value entails a duty of respect? And more precisely: would such duty of respect be *owed* to the work of art?

It seems that the correct answer is "No." The fact that an entity, x, bears non-instrumental (perhaps even non-comparative) value does not seem to entail that the fitting response to x is a stringent duty of respect owed to that being.

To see this, let me quickly introduce a distinction that I'll elaborate more fully in Section 2. There is an important contrast between simply having a duty period and a directed duty (a duty *owed* to a specific someone). This distinction parallels the contrast between doing something wrong and *wronging* a specific someone. And let's assume, for the sake of argument, that violating a directed duty *entails* wronging the party to whom the duty is owed.[8] For instance, if my duty not to assault you is *directed,* then I don't simply act wrongly in assaulting you, I also *wrong you.* By contrast, if my duty not to assault were not directed, my assault would not wrong you. You'd be, as Michael Thompson puts it, the *occasion* of my acting wrongly, but not my *victim* (Thompson 2004).

With this contrast in place, let's return to the David. Now, imagine that someone, thinking that portraying the David is pornographic, goes on a rampage and destroys Michelangelo and Bernini's David. The act would be abhorrent, bad, and maybe wrong in various ways. But now ask the key question: if there was a duty in the neighborhood here, was it *owed* to the David? More specifically: does the perpetrator violate a directed duty of respect owed to the David? It doesn't seem so. And further, it doesn't seem as if the act *violates the dignity* of the artistic artifact. Similarly, even if the perpetrator acts wrongly, it doesn't seem as if the perpetrator *wrongs* the David. These considerations suggest the following lesson: it's an open question whether such acts violate the dignity of the *David;* that is, it's intelligible to ask: "such acts are wrong and despicable, but do they violate the dignity of the *David*?"[9] But if it's an open question, this shows that the concept of non-instrumental value doesn't entail the concept of an obligation of respect owed to the bearer of such value.

Why does this matter? It matters greatly, for a simple reason: if Naturalist accounts analyze dignity in terms of a non-instrumental, non-relational value, since such value doesn't entail a stringent duty of respect owed to the bearer of such value, then Naturalist accounts have not met the Normativity Condition after all.[10]

To be clear: my point is not that naturalist accounts are hopeless. Instead, my point is only that naturalist accounts may find it more difficult to meet the normativity condition than it originally seems.

Let's turn now to the second condition concerning Recognition. Can Dignity Naturalism explain why the *misrecognition* of dignity matters in the distinctive way it does?

---

[8] As we'll see next, Nico Cornell has challenged the conceptual connection between wronging and claim-rights (2015). However, as far as I know, Cornell does not challenge the entailment from violation of a directed duty owed to *x,* to a *wrong to x.*

[9] I deliberatively make use of Moore's formulation of an open question argument here (Moore 1903), but in a very different way: not to show that the property of 'goodness' is primitive and unanalyzable, but to challenge the idea that directed deontic properties are included in purely evaluative ones. What I mean by "directed deontic properties" will become clearer in the next section.

[10] I develop this argument in more detail in Zylberman (2018).

To sharpen this question, notice there's a difference between the misrecognition of dignity simply mattering as something bad or wrong to do and misrecognition mattering more substantively as a *damage* or *diminishment*. The idea we presumably want to capture (or explain away) is why our dignity seems to be *vulnerable*, such that our misrecognition (or non-recognition) by others damages or diminishes our dignity in some important way.

Framed this way, Dignity Naturalism can seem to struggle with this condition. Since Dignity Naturalism conceives of dignity as an inherent and non-relational property, philosophers usually draw the implication that dignity is also *invulnerable,* that is, dignity itself cannot be damaged, changed, or affected in any way by relations of disrespect. But if fundamental dignity really is invulnerable, why does it matter if it's misrecognized – violated, attacked, undermined?

Philosophers who endorse Dignity Naturalism often seek a compromise here. The clearest articulation is probably due to Pablo Gilabert:

> condition-dignity is a state of affairs in which dignitarian norms are fulfilled.
> It concerns a more contingent situation human beings come to enjoy (and this
> includes certain treatment by others). (Gilabert 2019: 124)

Condition-Dignity is the state of affairs that obtains when others recognize or fail to recognize your fundamental dignity.

The distinction between fundamental and condition dignity prevents conceptual confusion, argues Gilabert (2019: 122). The distinction enables us to say of slaves or exploited workers in sweatshops, for instance, that their dignity is vulnerable insofar as their condition dignity is not observed and that their fundamental dignity is invulnerable insofar as it's an inherent, non-relational property possessed by the enslaved or exploited individual.

Gilabert's is an elegant way to meet the Recognition Condition. Nevertheless, many philosophers find the solution ultimately problematic. To elaborate their concerns, let's turn to what I'll call "conventionalist" approaches to fundamental dignity.

1.3 Dignity Conventionalism

As in the previous section, my aim in this section is to explain the family of views I'll call Dignity Conventionalism and to highlight some of their advantages and distinctive challenges.

Consider

Dignity Conventionalism. Fundamental dignity is the extrinsic and social value agents have when they are respected.

I've formulated Dignity Conventionalism to stand in clear opposition to Dignity Naturalism. This conceptual tidiness need not always obtain, since philosophers may mix and match different features of these views. With that said, for the sake of clarity, I think it is worth focusing on the more analytically pure version of Conventionalism, especially since philosophers opposed to naturalism certainly endorse a view along these lines. Let me explain it.

First, fundamental dignity is not an inherent property of agents but an extrinsic one, one that obtains when certain relations of respect and recognition are in place. As Colin Bird formulates the point, what I've called Naturalist views have a *reactive* view of respect: respect is a response or reaction that tracks the independent value of dignity. By contrast, what I'm calling Conventionalist views have a *performative* view of respect: respect is an attitude and relation to others that *confers* dignity upon them (Bird 2021: 115).

Second, if dignity is an extrinsic property that is conferred when others actually respect you, then dignity cannot be a non-relational property you have regardless of your relations to others. Instead, dignity becomes an essentially social property, namely, the value you have when others actually respect you.

As with its naturalist counterpart, Dignity Conventionalism is a capacious proposal, admitting a variety of specifications. For instance, some philosophers think of dignity as the progressive outgrowth of more traditional social systems of honor and rank. As Kwame Anthony Appiah (2011: 128, 220) or Jeremy Waldron (2012: 33) has put it, human dignity involves an "upwards equalization of [social] rank," so that we now accord to everyone the rank and social status that we used to attribute exclusively to nobility. Similarly, Suzy Killmister argues that social dignity consists in agents being able to uphold normative standards held by some social community or another. From there, we can extrapolate a conventionalist view of human dignity as a special type of social fact:

> I propose that it is a social fact about our current world that we have constituted a global community of human beings, and in doing so have created human dignity. (2017: 2078)[11]

On Killmister's view, then, human dignity is best understood as a kind of worth that is socially conferred and so extrinsic and dependent on social recognition.

Is Dignity Conventionalism true? I think a helpful way of understanding the main line of argument proponents defend is in terms of the two conditions we

---

[11] More recently, Killmister distinguishes social dignity (being held to the dignatarian norms of one's community) from status dignity (membership in a social category that calls for respect) (2020: 33).

stipulated previously. What speaks in favor of Dignity Conventionalism (proponents say) is that Naturalist views misunderstand the normativity of dignity and underestimate the importance of recognition.

Let's pause to reflect on the Naturalist thought that dignity is an inherent and non-relational property, one invulnerable to any fluctuations in social relations. What could this property be?

To put pressure on this way of understanding dignity, Bird develops a colorful analogy to economic value. One of the watersheds in economic theory was the rejection of the medieval, objectivist view of just price theory in favor of a subjectivist view, where economic value is a function of the actual *valuings* of individuals (2021: 69). Bird's analogy runs like this. Just like scholastic political thinkers analyzed the fairness of exchanges in terms of value properties inherent in objects (e.g., the economic value of this table is fixed objectively by its inherent properties), so too Naturalist views of dignity analyze the fairness of relations of respect in terms of the intrinsic, non-relational value of individuals. However, it is mysterious what kind of property the "real value" of objects could be if one abstracts from valuings and preferences of economic agents. Similarly, just as economic theory abandoned just price theory, so too the theory of dignity should abandon naturalism. It is less mysterious to understand the value of dignity as a result of complex social relations of actual respect.

The conclusion of this argument is that naturalist accounts misunderstand the role of recognition. Social recognition is not an accidental fact. Rather, the conventionalist argues for the much stronger view that, like economic value, dignity is a normative property that is *constituted* by social recognition.

A second argument follows from the first. Since the Naturalist misunderstands the role of recognition, the Naturalist makes it puzzling why we should care as much as we do about the *misrecognition* of fundamental dignity.

To bring out the idea, consider a thought experiment. Suppose your most treasured possession were a beautiful diamond you inherited from your grandparents. Suppose, further, that you were able to conjure up an enchantment such that a super-powerful demon made it metaphysically impossible for anyone to steal or even come within a foot of your diamond. If anyone (or anything) approached it, the moment they got to within three feet, the diamond would disappear to magically reappear firmly once again under your control. In short, it would be a metaphysically necessary fact that it's impossible to steal or damage the diamond –and, let's add, you had certain knowledge of this fact.

Nevertheless, in spite of this knowledge, you grow worried about this diamond being stolen or damaged and you spend countless resources to protect it. You build a fortress, you install security cameras and pay untold fortunes to security firms.

Does this make any sense? It doesn't. Your actions would manifest irrationality.

If you knew it's a metaphysically necessary fact that the diamond can't be stolen or damaged, why bother protecting it from theft or damage?

The thought experiment, I think, captures the crux of the conventionalist worry. Just like it makes no sense to protect from theft a diamond that can't be stolen, so too it makes no sense to protect from violation a normative property that is invulnerable. More pointedly, if dignity really is non-relational, inherent and invulnerable, the naturalist account appears powerless to explain why we care so deeply about misrecognition of our dignity through disrespect, humiliation, or violation.[12]

Notice that the thought experiment makes trouble for Dignity Naturalism even if it's equipped with Gilabert's distinction between fundamental and condition dignity. As Suzy Killmister argues, "Gilabert has the resources to say *that* certain acts damage dignity," but "his account struggles to explain *why*" (2017: 2068). Killmister's concern is that a naturalist account struggles to explain why recognition matters as deeply as it seems to – if the value that grounds recognition is perfectly impervious to fluctuations in treatment – much like your precious diamond.

There's more. There appears to be something important in the *phenomenology* of being wronged through misrecognition of one's fundamental dignity. When one is a victim of serious violation – enslavement, physical attack, assault – one has the feeling that one's dignity has been damaged, violated. And yet, if dignity truly is immutable and invulnerable, this feeling would be like an illusion. The worry, then, is that naturalist accounts misunderstand the role of recognition for a third kind of reason: they misconstrue the phenomenology of being wronged.

Having established that Dignity Naturalism fails to meet the Recognition Condition (let's grant for the sake of argument), the conventionalist can mount an argument to the conclusion that Naturalism also fails to meet the normativity condition.

The strategy, I take it, is to flip upside down the order of explanation. Abandon the project of grounding norms of respect in the value of dignity. Instead, dignity comes *after* respect. It is the value conferred on you by actual social relations of recognition and respect. And the account can meet the Deontic Normativity condition by showing respect is a different kind of attitude from those that are the fitting responses to other kinds of values, like the economic value of things.

---

[12] Bird presses what I take to be a similar line of argument (2021: 78).

For instance, Suzy Killmister distinguishes personal, social, and human dignity by the different types of norms that govern the construction of dignity (2017). More recently, Killmister distinguishes social dignity (being held to the dignatarian norms of one's community) from status dignity (membership in a social category that calls for respect) (2020: 33). The distinction enables Killmister to argue that human dignity is the distinctive status involved in membership in the social category human. Being human is not a natural, biological, or transcendental fact; it's a social one – like being a teacher or an Italian. The distinctive deontic normativity of dignity is explained by the norms of respect attached to this unique social fact, the fact that we've constructed the status of human dignity.

In sum, conventionalist philosophers argue that Naturalism misunderstands the significance of social recognition and thereby misconstrues the concept of dignity. Dignity is not an inherent non-relational property of individuals but is a social fact, a status *conferred* through social recognition.

1.4 An Impasse?

The trouble, I now suggest, is that Dignity Conventionalism faces mirroring difficulties of its own.

Though conventionalist views can appear to be recent in the literature, Thomas Hobbes articulated the basic contours of the view almost four hundred years ago, in 1651. In his celebrated *Leviathan*, Hobbes defines dignity as follows:

> The public worth of a man, which is the value set on him by the common-wealth, is that which men commonly call Dignity. And this value of him by the commonwealth, is understood, by offices of command, judicature, public employment; or by names and titles, introduced for distinction of such value. (x.18)

Hobbes's view is that an agent's dignity is constituted by how other agents actually value them, by what social positions are created in order to mark distinctions of such value. To be sure, Hobbes is tying here the concept of dignity to the concept of the state. But there is a short step from this view to the full-fledged conventionalist view of Waldron, Killmister, or Bird. To value a person highly is to respect them and so confer dignity on them. Conversely, to dishonor and disrespect them is to disvalue them, taking their public worth away.

Now, one worry with this line of thought is that it collapses the distinction between dignity and other forms of valuing – and especially economic valuing.

Steve Darwall presses this argument (Darwall 2017). Darwall notes that Hobbes himself frankly admits (Hobbes 1996):

> The value, or Worth of a man, is as of all other things, his price; that is to say, so much as would be given for the use of his power. (*Leviathan*, xx)

The worry is that if dignity is a conventional value set on persons by others, it's hard to see how dignity could entail norms with exigent normative grip. After all, the fact that your kitchen toaster commands a certain price in the market doesn't entail that its value generates an exigent normative demand of respect. You may, without moral compunction, throw out your old, broken toaster and replace it with a newer one. But we can't do that with persons. The conventionalist account seems unable to explain this difference.

Colin Bird argues that this type of objection is too quick. The Conventionalist view has the resources to make qualitative distinctions between market value and dignity. Bird's own view departs from Hobbes and insists that dignity differs from price by "independently expressed attitudes of respect for people and their lives" (2021: 128).

I'm not convinced. Darwall zooms in on the problem:

> Patterns of deference and respectful treatment constituting high status *de facto* entail nothing about how people in that position should be treated (*de jure*) or about normatively valid claims they might therefore have on others or others' correlative obligations to them. (2017: 187)

Admittedly, Darwall's objection can seem to beg the question, since it seems to require the premise that the exigent duty of respect must track a non-conventional value – the very naturalist premise rejected by the conventionalist.

But I think there's a way of framing Darwall's objection that is not question-begging. All we need is the neutral premise that social facts, as such, do not entail exigent normative duties of respect. For instance, the social fact that many felons in the United States are permanently deprived of rights doesn't establish that these individuals *should* be so deprived. The social fact that Jewish individuals were not allowed to lodge in certain hotels doesn't establish that such individuals *should* have been so excluded. And so on. But if social facts don't necessarily establish normative ones, then the social fact that x is conferred the social status of possessing dignity doesn't establish anything about dignity as a normative idea.

This worry is very important, so let me put it in a different way.[13] Ask: why should you respect others?

---

[13] I first elaborated this line of criticism of Bird's conventionalism in Zylberman (2022).

If the Conventionalist just takes the fact that you are respected as a brute social fact, that's hardly explanatory. There must be a good reason why others are owed your respect. But the performative view must be silent on such reasons, making the account at best opaque and at worst arbitrary.

Yet, there is a way for a conventionalist to explain why you have a duty to respect others. Consider the following remark from Colin Bird:

> "Devalorization" no more changes anyone's *value as a human being*, still less renders anyone worthless, than a restaurant's going bust establishes that it had no culinary merit. Indeed, devalorization tells us nothing about any one person as such. It is a condition in which the *value of human beings* loses any power to shape the attention and treatment they receive from others. Their *real worth* no longer makes any impact. (2021: 218)

Bird's response to the problem of normativity is straightforward: ultimately, you have a duty to respect others in virtue of their *value as a human being,* their *real worth.* This line of response is also inconsistent.

If respect is, after all, grounded in the value of human beings, then the performative view of respect collapses into the reactionary one. Respect tracks the value of human beings – and such value holds independently of valorization. To be sure, Bird is not using the term "dignity" to describe the "value of human beings," their "real worth." But this sounds awfully like what Naturalist philosophers would call fundamental dignity.

What begins to emerge is a serious dilemma for conventionalism. On the one hand, if dignity is no more than a social fact, then dignity is normatively empty. There are no reasons why you ought to respect others. (At least Hobbes's brutal view that your dignity is the public worth others assign you had the virtue of consistency.) On the other hand, if the conventionalist begins to tell a story that goes beyond sheer social facts – say, a story appealing to the "value of human beings," their "real worth" – then the conventionalist account might be able to explain the normativity of dignity – but only by presupposing the kind of dignity naturalism it was supposed to transcend. This is a serious dilemma: either conventionalism is explanatorily vacuous (because opaque or arbitrary) or it's able to explain dignity only by collapsing into a non-conventionalist account.[14]

We have now come full circle. The difficulties internal to Dignity Naturalism led us to consider Dignity Conventionalism. And yet, conventionalism faces a serious dilemma, potentially collapsing back into naturalism.

How to move forward?

---

[14] I deliberately use the term "serious" and refrain from saying "fatal'. There might be a way for the conventionalist to get out of this dilemma, but, at the very least, the path out is fraught with considerable obstacles.

One option is to try to render more sophisticated either of these explanatory strategies. Nothing in this section was offered as an argument to the conclusion that such refinements would be hopeless. And if you're so inclined, then this section can hopefully provide resources to calibrate more refined versions of these views.

My hunch is that a more promising strategy may be to try to extract an important lesson from the impasse itself in order to elaborate a genuine alternative.

Here's a possibility I'd like to explore. Notice that so far I've been able to recreate the main features of both types of analysis of fundamental dignity without appealing to the notion of a right. The notion of a right does not appear in either naturalist or conventionalist formulation. But what if that is a mistake? What if there is a much tighter conceptual connection between the very nature of dignity and that of rights?

Earlier, I brought up Brazilian philosopher Miguel Reale's question about value (whether Michelangelo or Bernini's David was more beautiful) to elucidate a subtle but important point. Unless one says more, the notion of value (even the notion of a non-instrumental value) does not appear to entail the deontic notion of an obligation owed to another.[15] This was my little "open deontic question" argument: "Sure, destroying Bernini's David is bad, but does it *wrong* the David?" If the question makes sense, it brings out the possibility that failure to appreciate the non-instrumental value of Bernini's David need not be a violation of the rights of the work of art.

These thoughts begin to open up a novel avenue of investigation.

The idea may be that dignity is a different kind of value because of Feinberg's idea: there's a conceptual connection between dignity (respecting a person) and respecting their rights. If so, what helps to explain the connection between dignity and the stringent duty of respect is precisely the conceptual connection fundamental dignity has to fundamental entitlements.

This line of thought would link the notion of fundamental dignity to the notion of rights, but what are rights anyway?

2 Rights: Between Naturalism and Conventionalism

The philosophical literature on the nature of rights has centered on a debate between two competing analyses: the primary function of rights is to protect interests (Interest) or to protect choices (Will). I then introduce a venerable

---

[15] To put the point more carefully: for the overall argument in this section to work, I only need the left to right entailment from dignity to a stringent duty of respect. I can remain agnostic on the right to left direction, that is, on whether *only* dignity entails stringent duties of respect. I thank an anonymous referee for pressing me to clarify this point.

tradition that analyzes rights in a manner analogous to Dignity Conventionalism. After introducing these standard views and their familiar difficulties, I hope to begin opening up conceptual space for an alternative, a task that will occupy me in the remaining two sections.

2.1 Preliminaries

Let's begin by introducing the notion of a right and some preliminary conditions of a philosophical account of rights.

First, a clarification of scope – parallel to the one in the previous section. My central topic is organized by the formal question: what are rights and why do they matter? To focus on this question I set aside substantive questions about who exactly has rights (individuals or groups? Only human animals or nonhuman animals as well?) or what specific rights they may have.

Let's refine the formal question further, given how widely the term "rights" is used. As Hillel Steiner has remarked, when it comes to contemporary rights theory the "beginning of wisdom . . . is widely agreed to be the classification of jural positions developed by Wesley Newcomb Hohfeld."[16] For our purposes, Hohfeld had two basic ideas: the ordinary use of the term "right" is ambiguous, and we can disambiguate this notion by noting that rights are inherently relational positions, each logically entailing a distinct correlate (typically in another person). Let me explain.

One of the central confusions Hohfeld attempted to avert is involved in the idea that all rights logically correlate with duties.[17] Though claim-rights do logically correlate with duties, other kinds of rights don't. To see this, consider

(1) Ahmed has a duty to pay Barack $50.
(2) Barack has a right, as against Ahmed, that Ahmed pay him $50.

Hohfeld's thought is that the right in (2) has a distinct structure: Barack has a *claim-right* against Ahmed. And this distinct structure is characterized by a distinct relationality: Barack has a claim-right *against* Ahmed. What makes the relation distinct is not just that Barack has this right exclusively against Ahmed (Barack doesn't have a claim-right, say, against you), it's also that, as Hohfeld would put it, the logical correlative of a claim-right is Ahmed's duty to

---

[16] Steiner (1994), quoted in Rainbolt (2006: 1). See Hohfeld (1919). For discussion, see (Kramer 1998), Rainbolt (2006: 1–19), Wenar (2013), D'Almeida (2016), Gilbert (2018), and Cruft (2019: 5–7, 80–3).

[17] "One of the greatest hindrances to the clear understanding, the incisive statement, and the true solution of legal problems frequently arises from the express or tacit assumption that all legal relations may be reduced to 'rights' and 'duties' . . . " (1919: 28).

Barack. Claim-rights, then, logically correlate with duties and, equivalently, duties logically correlate with claim-rights.

But not all rights have this structure. When we speak of rights, sometimes we have in mind what Hohfeld called "privileges." Consider:

(3) Chantal has a privilege as regards Barack not to pay Barack $50.

Chantal's privilege[18] is a right but doesn't correlate with a duty. In fact, a Hohfeldian privilege entails the absence of a duty. To say that Chantal has a privilege not to pay Barack is just to say that, unlike Ahmed, she does not stand under a duty to pay Barack $50. Thus, though the point is controversial, some think we can even say that a stapler has a privilege to staple papers (Rainbolt 2006: 8) or that, if it's true that your left shoe has no duties toward anything, then "your left shoe has privileges as regards everything" (Thomson 1992).

This distinction between rights as claims and rights as privileges matters for at least two reasons. One is conceptual clarity. The other is that claim-rights and privileges function differently, structuring different kinds of relations. To put this starkly, imagine a world that contained only privileges (maybe, a Hobbesian state of nature). This would be a world without duties. But if there are no duties, no one can do wrong – or wrong others.[19] To see this, insert Barack and Ahmed in our world containing only privilege-rights. The fact that Ahmed has a privilege to style his hair as he sees fit means that Barack can't violate Ahmed's rights by styling Ahmed's hair as Barack sees fit. After all, in this world, we've stipulated there are only privileges – and so no duties or claim-rights.

But the distinction matters for yet another reason. Privileges are not merely the absence of duties; they are also the presence of what we might call "bare permissions."[20] Suppose Barack is playing soccer on the street; his ball rolls into Ahmed's vast property; and we think "Barack has a right

---

[18] Most commentators render what Hohfeld calls privileges as "liberties," partly on the basis that Hohfeld's term is outdated. However, I have found that those new to the Hohfeldian framework tend to hear in the term "liberty" the presence of a claim-right to non-interference. Everyone is in agreement that a Hohfeldian privilege doesn't entail duties of non-interference and in fact entails only the absence of a duty. For similar reasons, Thomson preferred to keep the term "privilege" (1992: 53–4). I follow her lead here.

[19] I here make the widely held assumption that the category of a wrong presupposes the category of a duty. Nico Cornell (2015) has recently challenged this assumption. For powerful responses to Cornell, see Wallace (2019) and Cruft (2019).

[20] I call privileges 'bare permissions' to contrast such permissions with those that might be packaged into the concept of a claim-right. It's a contested issue whether claim-rights entail permissions. For instance, Kramer denies such entailment, while Steiner (2002) affirms it. To not get tangled up in the weeds, I bracket it here.

to pick up the ball from Ahmed's land." Here we may but need not think that Barack has a claim-right against Ahmed that Ahmed not interfere in Barack picking up the ball. Instead, we might just think that Barack has a bare permission to do so, that is, that he is not under a duty not to cross Ahmed's property line simply to pick up the ball. And such bare permissions, though thin, make important differences to the practical landscape, structuring things we may do – precisely because we stand under no duty not to do them.

With this primary distinction between claim-rights and privileges in place, let me quickly mention the other pair of distinctions made by Hohfeld. When we speak of rights, sometimes we refer to neither claims nor privileges but to what Matthew Kramer has labeled "second-order" normative positions: powers and immunities. Very roughly, you have a normative power when you have the ability to change claims, duties, or privileges, and you have immunities with regard to x when *others* lack powers to change your situation with regard to x. The correlative of a power is a *liability* (the position of vulnerability to deontic change), while the correlative of an immunity is a *disability* (the other party's lack of a power). An everyday but important example is your power to consent. When you sign a waiver before a surgery, you are in effect exercising your power to change the surgeon's standing duty not to assault you into a permission to cut you up. Crucially, powers don't correlate with duties either; they correlate with liabilities. A Hohfeldian liability need not be a bad thing – after all the surgery might be lifesaving. A Hohfeldian liability is just the position of vulnerability to deontic change.

Having distinguished these four concepts of rights, notice that claim-rights enjoy a certain priority. For one thing, claim-rights entail duties, while privileges entail the absence of duties. That means we can't fully comprehend the nature of a privilege without understanding what is supposed to be missing. For another, second-order relations (powers and immunities) depend on first-order relations like claim-rights. For these reasons, claim-rights have taken pride of place in the literature of rights. And I will follow this practice. This doesn't mean that the other relations are less important or don't add new dimensions to our understanding of rights. Far from it. But for reasons of space and considering the logical priority of claim-rights, that's the notion I'll focus on.

We may now sharpen our formal question: how should the idea of a claim-right be understood and justified (henceforth, unless otherwise specified, by "right" I shall mean "claim-right")?

It's also important to pause to clarify what one might expect from an answer. There are at least three important desiderata.

The first condition is

> *Extensional Adequacy*: A good analysis should explain (or explain away) most of our uses of the term "claim-right."

The language of claim-rights is extremely diverse in our everyday lives. Sometimes we use it to speak of momentous "moral" rights, such as your right not to be enslaved or deceived; sometimes we use this language to speak of socially specific rights, such as your right to a parking pass at work or your right to $200 when you cross the start line in the game Monopoly.

Let's call a second condition the

> *Relational Deontic Condition*: The concept of a claim-right entails a stringent duty of respect.

This condition is the parallel to the normativity condition of dignity. Just like dignity is supposed to entail stringent duties of respect, so too claim-rights logically correlate with duties. And as Hohfeld clarified, these duties are *directed,* owed to claim-right bearer. A good analysis of claim-rights should explain not just how rights generate reasons for action (think again of my reasons to get an espresso rather than fast-food drip coffee), but also how the reasons in question are *directed duties.*

And finally, we need to explain why claim-rights matter and so why misrecognition of claim-rights matters. Call this the Recognition Condition.

> *Recognition Condition*: The misrecognition and violation of claim-rights matters in distinctive ways and sometimes deeply.

Just as with dignity, a good analysis of rights should explain why claim-rights can seem so vulnerable to damage, violation, and misrecognition.

In sum, a good answer to our question (how should claim-rights be understood and justified?) will be extensionally adequate, explain why rights correlate with directed duties, and why the misrecognition of claim-rights (through disrespect, violation, etc.) matters as distinctively and deeply as it seems to.

2.2 Interest and Will Theories

The contemporary philosophical literature on rights contains two main families of answers: Interest and Will theories. In examining these views, I proceed fairly quickly because the theories and their distinctive challenges are well understood in the literature. For now, I don't advance novel lines of objection.

Let's start with Interest. The basic idea is that the function of rights is to protect the interests of right-holders. There are two main versions of Interest theory I'm aware of, one is justificatory, the other non-justificatory. The justificatory version construes the notion of entailment substantively; that is, interests *explain* or *justify* why we have duties (and rights). The non-justificatory version construes the notion of entailment conceptually; that is, interests do not explain or justify duties. Instead, granted that there are duties in a given normative domain, interests help us to *identify* which are the right-holders correlative to the duty. I discuss the justificatory version first, then turn to the non-justificatory one.

Begin with

> **Interest**: Agent *A* has a claim-right against *B* that B (not) φ if, and only if, B's duty derives from *A's* central interests.[21]

Interest says that certain aspects of your well-being are sufficiently important so as to *generate* (explain, justify) duties on others. To be sure, not every interest of yours is meant to attract the protection of a claim-right: hence the qualification to "central" interests.

Proponents argue that Interest meets our conditions. They claim the analysis is extensionally adequate. The analysis explains the significance and relationality of rights in terms of right-bearer's interests. And rights and their recognition matter because their violation is tantamount to setting back the interests of rights-bearer.

However, opponents argue that Interest fails on all three counts.

First, they argue that Interest is extensionally inadequate, for it can be both under- and over-inclusive.

Interest can be under-inclusive by leaving out clear cases of claim-rights that don't derive from the protection of right-bearer's interests. As Leif Wenar formulates the worry, Interest requires that all rights map the true interests of human beings, but this is implausible (2013: 205). As Wenar points out, in some societies parents have a right to arrange the marriage of their children – and children a duty to abide by their decisions. But this statement would be true even if it were also true that human beings who are parents are normally better off when parents lack a legal right to arrange marriages (Wenar 2013: 205). More generally, Interest struggles with a plethora of conventional rights that appear to be disconnected from the interests of individuals.[22]

---

[21] There are various formulations of the view. An early and influential formulation is due to Raz (1986). A recent defense of the justificatory version is offered by May (2012; 2017). Similar formulations have been elaborated by Waldron (1993) and Fabre (2006). As Cruft notes (2019: 14), structurally similar theories might not place *interests* at the basis of rights, but still ground rights in values intelligible independently of rights. For instance, Griffin seeks to explain human rights in terms of the value of normative agency (2008); Nussbaum assigns capabilities the role of the value (2007); and Beitz's practice-based account of human rights is built on the Razian model (Beitz 2009).

[22] Rowan Cruft (2019: ch. 2) forcefully presses the objection that Interest is an inadequate analysis of many conventional rights, since these rights need not map the interests of human beings.

Interest can be over-inclusive by counting as rights cases where the protection of important interests is at stake – yet no rights seem to be in the offing. The standard difficulty, initially raised by H.L.A. Hart (1955), concerns third-party beneficiaries. Suppose that I hire you to renovate my kitchen and that you were going to donate most of your income on this job to a nonprofit seeking to promote food security. But I renege on our agreement, depriving the nonprofit from its anticipated donation. Here, my actions have set back the interests of a third party (the nonprofit) and, more importantly, of a fourth (the nonprofit's clients). Yet, though I've wronged you, the contractor, it's not clear I've violated the rights of the nonprofit or its clients – even if I've set back their interests.[23]

These extensional difficulties betray a deeper difficulty concerning the second condition of normativity. The worry is now familiar from the previous section: in general, evaluative facts don't seem to suffice to generate deontic ones. Applied to the topic of rights, the worry is this: the fact that some interest is furthered or set back doesn't entail facts about claim-rights. Sometimes a right can be violated without setting back any aspects of your well-being. For instance, you could break a promise to me, violating my promissory right, but, as it turns out, your breaking the promise was beneficial to me – say, I didn't have to eat at the restaurant I hate but that we had agreed to go together. Conversely, sometimes aspects of your well-being can be promoted without generating any rights. For instance, you could stand to seriously benefit by my tidying up your extremely messy and disorganized office without that generating any duties on others to help you tidy up your office.[24]

The deeper difficulty: there is at best a contingent connection between evaluative facts pertaining to your interests and deontic facts about rights.

Moreover, these difficulties carry over to the third condition. If there is indeed only a contingent connection between evaluative interests and deontic rights,

---

[23] The third-party beneficiary problem has been extensively discussed in the literature, and tracking the debate would take us too far afield. For instance, Kramer seeks to solve it by modifying "Bentham's test," in his formulation, the idea that if a detriment to A is *sufficient* to establish a breach by the duty-bearer, then A holds a correlative claim-right and otherwise not (1998: 81). Bentham's test *might* solve the problem. For instance, Kramer could argue that detriment to the nonprofit is not sufficient to establish breach by duty-bearer, while detriment to the contractor is sufficient. In response, Sreenivasan has argued that, though able to rule out some third-party beneficiaries, the Interest account is still unable to offer a principled distinction between the right-bearer (e.g., the promisee) and other related beneficiaries. For this reason, Sreenivasan concludes that the third-party beneficiary is "fatal" to Interest theory (2017: 145). In response, McBride (2020) and Kurki (2021) have developed sophisticated elaborations of the Bentham test that, they argue, effectively solves the objection from third-party beneficiaries.

[24] I owe this example to Jason D'Cruz.

that suggests that Interest misdiagnoses the significance of rights recognition. Put bluntly, if the main function of rights is not to protect independently intelligible interests, then the main significance of misrecognition can't just be that misrecognition sets back interests.

Interest theorists do have a powerful strategy to circumvent these difficulties: shift from the justificatory version to a non-justificatory version, perhaps, as follows:

> **Interest***: Agent A has a claim-right against B that B (not) φ only if (i) there is a duty in a given normative domain and (ii) upholding such duty is typically beneficial for beings like A. (Kramer 2017: 49)

Interest* makes three important modifications to Interest. Its main defender has been Matthew Kramer, so I'll take his variant as representative (1998, 2017). First, Kramer formulates only a necessary condition for right-holding, refraining from specifying sufficient conditions.[25] Second, this version of Interest theory is not justificatory: it does not seek to derive or justify duties. Instead, it grants that a certain duty exists (i) and then offers a necessary condition for *identifying* the relevant right-holders.[26] The third important innovation is that it doesn't say that rights *always* serve the interests of right-holders. Instead, it weakens the condition to say that rights are "generally advantageous" to right-holders (Kramer 1998: 96).

Although Interest* may fare better than the standard version, it still can seem liable to counter-examples. Wenar insists that parents may still have a legal right to marry their children even if it is not typically beneficial for parents to possess such a right.[27] Kramer has argued that such a right might be better analyzed either as a privilege (a parent stands under no duty not to select a marriage partner for their grown child) or as a power (the ability to change the child's normative situation), but not as a claim-right (2017: 69). Even if Kramer is correct, it seems similar counter-examples can arise. Suppose there is a jurisdiction that grants citizens a legal claim-right to purchase and possess any type of drug, including cocaine, heroin, or fentanyl. Here there would be a legal duty borne by other private individuals and public authorities not to interfere with an individual's purchase and use of hard drugs; and such duty would correlate with a legal right even if such right is *not typically beneficial*

---

[25] For Kramer's rationale, see Kramer (2017: 54).

[26] For Kramer's distinction between justificatory and non-justificatory versions, see Kramer (2017: 50, 56, 79).

[27] Kramer responds to this counter-example (2017: 69) by suggesting that, *if* there are such rights, they may be better understood as liberties or powers rather than claim-rights.

for the right-bearer, say, because access to purchase and use of such drugs is typically *destructive* of one's life.[28]

The deeper problem remains: the satisfaction of interests does not appear to be even a necessary condition of rights.

Opponents argue that if we shift to a Will theory of rights, these difficulties can be avoided. Here's a preliminary formulation:

> **Will.** Agent A has a claim-right against B that B (not) φ if, and only if, A has *normative control* over B's duty.

The basic idea: the core of a claim-right is an agent's normative control over a sphere of action and so over the duties of others concerning that sphere. While Interest thinks of right-bearers as passive recipients of well-being, Will thinks of right bearers as having active control.

There are important local disagreements about the character of the normative control required for rights.[29] Some think it involves a power of waiver (Hart 1955; Steiner 1994, 2002); or a power to demand the fulfillment of duty (Feinberg 1970; Darwall 2006, 2013; Skorupski 2010; Gilbert 2018); or a power to demand justification for its violation (Forst 2011); or a power to forgive its violation (Darwall 2006; Owens 2012; Jonker 2020); or some combination. I bracket these disagreements to focus on the abstract formula, Will.

Proponents argue that Will can meet our three conditions more successfully than Interest.

First, Will (we are told) is more extensionally adequate. Will handles better the counter-examples to Interest because Will makes interests neither necessary nor sufficient for rights. For instance, if parents have a right to marry off their children, that's simply because they have normative control over the duties of others.[30] Will avoids the problem of third-party beneficiaries. The fact that our agreement benefits a third party doesn't tell us anything about whether a third party has rights. If the third party (e.g., the nonprofit) lacks normative control over duties, then the third party lacks the relevant rights.

---

[28] To be clear, the jury is still out on extensional adequacy. So I don't mean to suggest that these counter-examples are fatal. They need not be. For instance, May (2017) and Kramer (2017) provide thoughtful and ingenious rebuttals to each of Wenar's alleged counter-examples. As we'll see next, the main issue I'll find with Interest in any version is not extensional adequacy but whether the account can have extensional adequacy while continuing to provide a reductive analysis. I'll turn to this key issue in the next section.

[29] What follows is Cruft's helpful taxonomy of Will (2019: 32).

[30] Though it should be noted that this example can, on reflection, cause trouble for Will. If the point of rights is to protect autonomy, how can there be a right to marry off other competent adults? I'm grateful to an anonymous referee for highlighting this difficulty.

Similarly, Will (we are told) has a better explanation of the normativity of rights. Rights matter because they protect the normative control and so the autonomy of agents. Conversely, violations of rights are violations of sovereign autonomy.

It seems, then, that Will meets our three theoretical conditions. What's not to like?

Well, Will, in fact, has serious difficulties of its own.

The extensional difficulties stem from cases where it seems plausible to say that an individual has claim-rights and yet said individual lacks normative control.[31]

One reason an individual might lack such normative control is that they are in a coma or are too young. Yet, it's not clear that such individuals must lack claim-rights. To see this, think of Margo, a two-year-old. It's implausible to hold that Margo has any version of normative control favored by Will theorists. Yet, it's also implausible to hold that Margo lacks rights. For instance, if Margo's parents neglect to feed them out of indifference, you'd likely say that the parents are violating Margo's rights to their care. But that's precisely the thought Will theorists can't make intelligible. Since Margo lacks normative control, Margo can't have claim-rights and so can't be wronged. This jars.

The difficulty is not restricted to two-year-olds. It extends to any individual who seemingly has claim-rights and yet lacks normative control: some adults; very young human beings; and possibly every nonhuman animal. If these individuals lack normative control, they can't have rights. That jars.

How can proponents of Will respond? A promising option is to claim that a person can exercise normative powers *on behalf of* another. H.L.A. Hart recoiled from his earlier denial that young children do not have Will theory rights by proposing that "where infants or other persons not *sui iuris* have rights, such powers ... are exercised *on their behalf* by appointed representatives ..." (Hart 1982). Similarly, Stephen Darwall argues that even if nonhuman animals lack the second-personal competence to demand the enforcement of duties from others, we might still ascribe rights to them insofar as *we* can place such demands on their behalf (2006: 29).

To assess this line of response, let me try to formulate it more abstractly:

> **Will***: Agent *A* has a claim-right against *B* that B (not) φ if, and only if, *either* (i) B's duty derives from *A's normative control* over B's duty, *or* (ii) *B*'s duty derives from a third party, *C,* who exercises normative control *on behalf of* A.

Though initially promising, Will* faces two serious challenges.

---

[31] This difficulty also affects, presumably the "hybrid" theory propounded by Sreenivasan (2005), which makes possession of the power of waiver necessary for possession of rights.

First, it appears to be false. Suppose I demand on behalf of the Hudson River that you stop throwing your garbage in it. Or suppose that I demand that you don't burn the Mona Lisa to keep warm during a cold night in an abandoned Louvre. It doesn't seem to follow that the Hudson has a claim-right against you polluting it or the Mona Lisa a claim-right against you burning it. To be sure, your actions might be wrong, but it's not obvious that your actions *wrong* the river or the work of art. More precisely, my normative control over your duty, even if exercised on behalf of another, *c,* does not *guarantee* that *c* has a correlative claim-right. If so, (ii) of Will* doesn't capture a sufficient condition for rights for those on whose behalf agents may act.

Second, suppose Will* is true. Still, it has an implausible implication: it entails that the third party has a right as well. Will says that normative control is a necessary and sufficient condition for having a right (and (i) of Will* preserves that bit of the analysis). But if third parties can truly exercise normative control on your behalf, that means that their normative control over the duties of others also gives *them* a right. Yet, that seems strange and implausible.

Here's how Cruft puts the point:

> When a passer-by demands that a farmer fulfil her duty of care to her cows (perhaps they are being abused), the duty is not owed to the passer-by even though she holds this power to demand its fulfilment. (Cruft 2019: 34–5)

Cruft's diagnosis gets to the heart of the problem. Will* seems to lack the conceptual resources to explain why the exercise of normative control gives one rights in some cases (when exercised on one's own behalf) but not in others (when exercised on behalf of others) (Cruft 2019: 35).[32] To be sure, one could simply stipulate this away, indicating that only exercising powers on one's own behalf is sufficient for claim-rights. But that would beg the key question: why does one kind of normative control confer rights on oneself but not on another (and vice versa)?

A further amendment of Will might still work, perhaps:

> **Will+:** Agent *A* has a claim-right against *B* that *B* (not) φ if, and only if, B's duty derives from *A's normative control* over B's duty. But if C exercises normative control on behalf of *A,* B's duty is owed to *C,* not *A.*

Will+ appears to be Hillel Steiner's strategy:

> What scintilla of a practical or analytical difference can it make if we construe the rights correlative to those protection duties as ones held *by those power-possessors* rather than ones held by unempowerable creatures? As far as I can see, none. (Steiner 2002: 261)

---

[32] Cruft also raises a similar problem in Cruft (2017: 170–2).

Steiner's article predates Cruft's objection by almost two decades. But here is how Will+ works: it bites the bullet. The underlying idea is that if an agent truly has normative control over another's duty, it is the agent who exercises that control that has the right – not the party on whose behalf agent acts. When you advocate on behalf of the Hudson River or the Mona Lisa, it is *you* who has a right, not the river or the art work. When you demand of the farmers that they be more caring of cows, it is *you* who exercises a right – not the cows. And Steiner's point is sharp: what scintilla of practical difference can it make if it's you who has the right rather than the Hudson, the Mona Lisa, or the cows?

However, Will+ has a troubling implication.

Suppose we make the widely held assumption that a necessary condition of wronging an individual A is that wrongdoer has a preexisting directed duty to A. Further, this is a supposition that Will theorists don't typically reject. But it has the following implication: in cases of breach, Will+ radically misdiagnoses the victim.

Let me illustrate by returning to Margo, our two-year-old. In this case, Will+ would say that it's not Margo who exercises normative control but a third party acting on her behalf, say, the local public authorities. The key implication of this analysis is that if the parents have a duty of care, that duty is owed to the public authority, *not to Margo!* The parents do not (and cannot!) wrong Margo. This jars.

In sum, Will says that normative control is the property that explains claim-rights and directed duties. But this property appears to be neither necessary nor sufficient for claim-rights. It's not necessary insofar as it seems possible for the comatose, very young humans or nonhuman animals to possess rights even if they lack normative control. And it's not sufficient because individuals can exercise normative control on behalf of others – but, contrary to Will+, that doesn't mean those exercising normative control have claim-rights. If so, any version of Will considered here struggles to explain the notion of a claim-right.

If both standard theories, Interest and Will, face such stubborn difficulties, how to move forward?

One possibility is to continue to refine the standard analyses. I've already pointed out one refinement of Interest (Interest*) and two of Will (Will* and Will+). But there is plenty of scope for ingenuous analytical refinement.

Another possibility would be to explore an account that departs from both Interest and Will.[33] Before introducing the alternative I find most promising, let

---

[33] For reasons of space, I cannot discuss these alternatives here. As far as I can tell, the main alternatives have been the hybrid view proposed by Sreenivasan (2005, 2017) and McBride (2017); the second-personal account developed by Cruft (2019); and the kind-desire theory developed by Leif Wenar (2013). Margaret Gilbert's important treatise on rights (2018) seeks to move beyond these familiar debates as well, but her account in terms of joint commitments

me discuss first a model of rights that parallels the conventionalist account of dignity.

2.3 Rights Conventionalism

To start articulating a conventionalist view, recall the passage from Hobbes I quoted in the previous section:

> The public worth of a man, which is the value set on him by the commonwealth, is that which men commonly call Dignity. (*Leviathan*, x.18)

Hobbes's view appears to be that absent the social recognition of the commonwealth – that is, in the state of nature – individuals have at best what Hohfeld called "privileges." The state of nature, then, is characterized not by claim-rights but by their absence.

One way to capture Hobbes's metaphysical thesis is as follows: claim-rights appear in the world not through isolated properties of individuals (their interests or choices) but through social properties and relations, such as agreements. Claim-rights are *created* by the agreement that constitutes the commonwealth.

Now this view seems limited and false. Surely the notion of a claim-right doesn't presuppose actual conferral by a Hobbesian state?

But if the Hobbesian version is limited, there's a simple extension of the view:

> **Rights Conventionalism:** Non-relational properties of agents are not sufficient for the existence of claim-rights. Rather, claim-rights are fixed by social acts of conferral and/or acknowledgment.

The general conventionalist idea is that no matter how fine-grained our story might be about the monadic, non-relational properties of individuals (e.g., their interests or choices), such properties are not enough to put claim-rights in place. Instead, rights appear in the world only through social facts of recognition.

Hobbes's Dutch predecessor, Hugo Grotius, articulated the point nicely in 1625, when he explained the right to property as follows:

---

seems to me to ultimately commit her to some version of Will discussed here – thereby replicating the same difficulties. At the same time, aspects of Gilbert's view (especially her connecting demand rights to agreements) can bring Gilbert's view closer to the conventionalist accounts I explain next. To that extent, Gilbert's account will inherit the virtues and the vices of such conventionalist accounts. I lack space to adequately address Cruft's account. But an underlying worry is that Cruft remains committed to an Interest view of rights – at least as far as natural rights are concerned. And if Interest fails as an analysis of natural rights, then so does Cruft's view. I discuss Wenar's Kind-Desire view in the final section.

And thus we learn how things became property; not by an act of the mind alone: for one party could not know what another party wished to have for its own, so as to abstain from that; and several parties might wish for the same thing; but *by a certain pact*, either express, as by division, or tacit, as by occupation. (Grotius 1625: Book II, §2)

Grotius's idea is that property rights are the *product of social conventions,* a "certain pact." Take away the social convention and the right vanishes.

Now, there is some scholarly controversy as to whether Grotius held a conventionalist view of all rights or only of some (Tuck 1979, 1999; Schneewind 1997; Irwin 2008; Darwall 2013). But that need not detain us.

What interests me is the general thesis of Rights Conventionalism, which, in effect, expands the Grotian view of property rights to *all* claim-rights.

More recently, Rex Martin has defended a version of Rights Conventionalism. Here is Martin:

to talk of rights of a wholly and permanently isolated individual [is probably pointless] . . . I want, rather, to suggest that this factor of social recognition or ratification is actually a constituent of rights – that is, of our characterization of something as a right. (1993: 27)

Martin's idea is that the natural, pre-conventional properties of individuals are not sufficient to explain what I've called the Relational Deontic structure of claim-rights. A better explanation is that certain monadic features (such as interests or choices) amount to rights only when socially established ways of acting establish norms for the protection of such interests.

After all, this was Grotius's insight. Absent the pact or convention, your interests in being able to control material objects in the world do not amount to a property right. However, once an agreement (explicit or implicit) is in place, the agreement puts in place directed duties and so generates, for the first time, a property right.[34]

To see this, imagine that you live with a group of friends. Nobody wants to live covered in garbage. But who ought to take the garbage out? Absent some kind of explicit or implicit convention, no one owes it to any other roommate to take out the garbage. But once you all agree, say, on a weekly rotation, each owes it to the rest to take out the garbage on certain weeks. And if the

---

[34] Earlier, I said that Margaret Gilbert's demand theory of rights might be understood as a specification of Will. She's often read as such (e.g., by Cornell 2019). However, the deeper idea Gilbert is after may be more like Grotius and Hobbes rather than Hart and Steiner. In making joint commitments the key explanans of agreements and so of rights, Gilbert seems to be developing a version of Rights Conventionalism. Regardless of the correct interpretation of Gilbert's sophisticated view, I think this is another virtue of transposing the taxonomy of naturalism and conventionalism from the theory of dignity to the theory of rights: it gives us the vocabulary to enrich our thinking about the nature of claim-rights.

convention puts in place a directed duty, since directed duties logically correlate with claim-rights, the agreement also puts in place claim-rights.

It's important to highlight what's distinctive about Rights Conventionalism. To be sure, Interest and Will, in principle, can distinguish between moral, legal, and political rights and analyze the latter as being conventional. So the point of contrast is *not* whether the standard theories can accommodate conventional rights: they can. Instead, the issue is seen most clearly by focusing on moral rights. Darby puts the point crisply:

> I believe that there are no rights that exist prior to and independent of social recognition of ways of acting and being treated. So insofar as natural rights, human rights, and presocial moral rights are understood in this manner, my thesis is that there simply are no such rights. (Darby 2009: 1)

Whereas the standard models need not deny the intelligibility of "natural, human, and presocial moral" rights, Rights Conventionalism holds that such rights not only do not exist, but also that the very concept of such rights is unintelligible. That's because the very concept of a right makes reference to social recognition. And that thesis is much stronger than anything standard Interest and Will theorists typically adopt.

Conventionalist philosophers argue that their analysis can meet our three theoretical conditions.

First, Conventionalism can meet the recognition condition. Recognition matters, as Hobbes and Grotius put it, because social recognition *creates* the rights in the first place. Conversely, if you take away social recognition, then the rights disappear from view.

Second, proponents argue that Conventionalism can explain the distinctive, relational normativity of rights. Instead of trying to derive relational norms (directed duties or claim-rights) from non-relational values of interests or choices, Rights Conventionalism explains relational normativity as constitutive of specific, actual agreements or conventions.

Third, conventionalism can offer a distinctive solution to the problem of extensional fit. Remember, both Interest and Will struggle to get the correct extensional fit. By contrast, Derrick Darby states:

> there appear to be no fixed limits on the kinds of beings that could possess legal rights ... since this status is not tied to the nature of things, right-conferring authorities can extend this status to whom or whatever they choose. (2009: 99)

Darby's thought, I take it, is that since non-relational features of individuals are neither necessary nor sufficient for rights, there are no ontological constraints on what type of being can bear rights. Babies, the dead, flags, AI personal assistants? No problem. What matters is that the relevant practices of rights-conferral be in place.

Darby's may be an elegant solution to the problem of extension. While Interest struggles with conventional rights that don't seem to benefit right-holders (e.g., legal rights to marry one's children or to purchase and use hard drugs), Conventionalism accommodates such rights with ease – since they are the paradigm form of rights. And while Will struggles with individuals who lack normative control, such lack is no barrier to the possession of conventional rights – since in principle any being can have rights.

In sum, not only does Rights Conventionalism have a venerable historical pedigree, it also appears to be a robust and promising alternative to the more familiar analyses.

Nevertheless, I think that rights conventionalism inherits the same structural challenges as conventionalist views of dignity. In particular, Rights Conventionalism, I argue, faces a trilemma of normativity: either it's unable to explain the *normativity* of rights, or if it can bring in normative notions, it's unable to explain *rights,* or even if it can accommodate the normativity of rights, it's unable to explain an important category of *wrongs.*

Begin with the first prong of the trilemma: normativity. To bring the problem into view, let's disambiguate Rights Conventionalism:

Simple Rights Conventionalism. Social facts (pertaining to conventions, recognition, conferral and/or acknowledgment) are in themselves sufficient for claim-rights.

This variant of conventionalism is ultra-minimalist about the normative, explaining rights reductively in terms of social facts of recognition and acknowledgment. For example, to say that you have a property right to your smartphone is just to say that you live in a society that typically acknowledges such a claim.

But such minimalism may be too minimalist. As a general matter, it's not clear that social facts alone are sufficient to fix normative facts. Stephen Darwall, as we saw, makes this point as an objection against conventionalist views of dignity. It's worth re-stating Darwall's objection:

Even if certain rights and privileges were themselves part of an honored status, nothing would follow about whether these rights and privileges *should* be honored with the kind of respect that helps constitute the rights-including status as a social fact. (Darwall 2017: 188)

Remember: there's a way of construing Darwall's objection in a question-begging way. Here, one could worry that Darwall's objection presupposes the very pre-conventional rights the conventional theorist denies. But there's also a non-question-begging way of construing the objection. As earlier, all we need is the uncontroversial idea that some conventions are wrong and should not be honored. And if so, the social fact that *x* is an established way of acting or of being treated doesn't suffice to establish the normativity of a right, that is, to establish that these rights and privileges *should* be respected. For example, the social fact that you live in a sexist society that grants males certain rights and privileges advantaging them over women and gender nonconforming individuals doesn't establish the existence of such rights and privileges. If Darwall's objection is on point, it carries over to Simple Rights Conventionalism: such an account fails to explain the normativity of rights.

Nevertheless, conventionalist views have a ready line of response available. Proponents can argue that the most plausible version of rights conventionalism isn't Simple but

> **Sophisticated Rights Conventionalism**: *A* possesses moral right *R* if, and only if, (i) *A*'s acting in a certain way or being treated in a certain way is *socially established* (formally and/or informally), *and* (ii) *A*'s action or way of being treated is *morally justified*.[35]

Unlike the Simple variant, the Sophisticated Variant denies that social facts suffice for normative facts about rights and holds that, at least for moral rights, a normative property is necessary.

I think Sophisticated Rights Conventionalism avoids the sting of the no normativity objection, but only by being pushed into a different problem, namely, its inability to explain rights. Why?

The second component of the Sophisticated variant must involve some normative notion, but such notion *cannot* be the notion of a right on pain of circularity. Darby sees the difficulty: if the notion of moral justification in (ii) appealed to the notion of some basic rights, then the account would not explain but presuppose rights.[36] Call this the "no circularity" condition.

The trouble, then, is that if the no circularity condition is satisfied, the conventionalist analysis, no matter how sophisticated, doesn't yield rights.

To see this, let's try to develop the sophisticated conventionalist analysis of a child's moral right to education. Roughly, the analysis would run as follows:

> *Right to Education*: *A* possesses a moral right to education *Re* if, and only if,
> (i) *A*'s free access to quality elementary education is socially established

---

[35] I think something like this view is endorsed by Derrick Darby in his analysis of moral rights. See Darby (2009: 86–90).

[36] 'it would be circular to reintroduce basic moral rights to specify the shape of the justification conferring moral principles' (Darby 2009: 89).

(formally and/or informally), and (ii) *A*'s access to quality elementary education is *morally justified.*[37]

To be sure, an individual's right to education includes far more than just access to free elementary education. But for the purposes of illustration, suppose this is the exhaustive content of the right. The difficulty is that these two conditions can be satisfied without amounting to a right.

Suppose that there is a socially established norm, recognized by the government, that as a matter of good Christian charity, the wealthy should donate sufficient money to an education fund such that every child in that society can access quality elementary education for free. Further, suppose that there is a good moral justification for this imperfect duty of charity on the wealthy. In this society, I contend, the two conditions of Sophisticated Rights Conventionalism can be satisfied without giving any child a right to education. At best, what this analysis of Right to Education yields is the existence of a social policy to provide access to a service. But the existence of this policy doesn't necessarily confer rights on anyone.

But what is true of this faulty analysis of Right to Education is also true of Sophisticated Rights Conventionalism *as such.* The fact that its two conditions are satisfied doesn't guarantee the existence of a right. If so, the Sophisticated variant might avoid the problem of normativity affecting its Simple cousin, but only by succumbing to a problem of "no rights."

These difficulties bring into the open a deeper one: Conventionalist accounts struggle to explain the normativity of rights.

To bring the issue into focus, return to the notion of wrongs and consider this argument:

> *P.1. Wrongs*: An agent *A* wrongs another, *B,* only if *A* owes a duty to *B* and *A* violates that duty.
>
> *P.2. Hohfeldian Correlativity*: *A*'s directed duty to *B* that *A* (not) φ is logically equivalent to *B*'s claim-right that *A* (not) φ.
>
> *No right → no wrong conclusion*. Therefore, if *B* doesn't have a claim-right that *A* (not) φ, then *B* is not wronged by *A*'s φing.

P1 captures the plausible and widely held view that a preexisting directed duty is a necessary condition of wronging another. P2 captures the widely held view that claim-rights logically correlate with directed duties. But when put together, they entail that if in certain conditions individuals lack rights, they can't be wronged.

---

[37] I think something like this view is endorsed by Derrick Darby in his analysis of moral rights. See Darby (2009: 86–90).

Let me illustrate the No Wrongs argument. Consider the Dred Scott Decision (1857). Suppose that this decision provides sufficient epistemic warrant for establishing that, circa 1857 in the United States, it was a social fact that Black individuals had no socially established rights. Now, let's analyze this in terms of the No Wrongs Argument. First, given (P.2. Hohfeldian Correlativity) the fact that no Black individual had claim-rights establishes that no one owed any duties correlative to such claim-rights. However, given (1. Wrongs), if no one owed any duties to Black individuals, then no one could wrong (or at least no one did wrong) Black individuals. This leads to the No Rights → No Wrongs conclusion: since Black individuals had no rights (in any sense) circa 1857 in the United States, it follows that no Black individual was wronged, in spite of the horrific conditions of slavery. This implication jars.

In response to this type of worry, Darby concedes that denying natural rights can seem wrong. Yet, instead of saying that Black individuals had their natural rights violated, we should say that such individuals *"ought* to have rights," but they don't (Darby 2009: 92–3). Shifting the semantics of rights statements from a description of the rights individuals have to an expression of support for the rights they ought to have is an ingenious move.

Nevertheless, it still seems to me that this conventionalist maneuver fails to deal with the underlying problem. So long as the two minimalist premises of the No Wrongs arguments hold (and conventionalists provide no independent argument against them), it also follows that no Black individual was wronged by slavery. This result seems to me conceptually and morally problematic.

Let us take stock. In the current section, we began with the opposition between the two dominant analyses of rights, Interest and Will. After exploring some refinements and their familiar difficulties, I introduced a conventionalist alternative stemming from Grotius and Hobbes to the contemporary work of Rex Martin, Derrick Darby (and perhaps Margaret Gilbert). While conventionalist views seem to be able to accommodate the cases left out by the standard models, they also inherit a trilemma of normativity parallel to the one we encountered in section 1, now the trilemma of *no normativity, no rights,* or *no wrongs.*

3 Natural Rights: A Kind-Dispositional Model

The first half of this Element examined familiar accounts of dignity and rights, highlighting both their explanatory virtues and distinctive liabilities. One option for moving forward is simply to finesse such accounts. But in the second half, I begin to explore an alternative that seeks to vindicate Feinberg's idea that dignity and rights are interdependent notions.

To do so, I introduce two new ideas. First, I suggest that many of the difficulties of the familiar accounts can be traced to a metaphilosophical commitment to a reductivist and atomist model of explanation. Accordingly, I begin to explore the alternative: a non-reductivist and holistic model of explanation. Second, such a model draws from a metaphysics of kinds and dispositions to illuminate how dignity and rights function as *normative* kinds and dispositions: dignity is a distinctive form of goodness attaching to kinds and necessarily connected to rights, and rights encode specific ways of acting or being treated that, through recognition, actualizes dignity. The basic idea is that dignity and rights are dynamic relational properties: in their natural guise, they exist independently of conventional recognition, yet they are actualized or completed through relations of recognition. Accordingly, I argue, the emerging model can explain the interdependence of dignity and rights and meet the demands of recognition and normativity. The current section begins to develop the model for natural rights; the next one for socially constituted ones.

3.1 Reductivism and Atomism

As divergent as the literatures on dignity and rights are, many of the difficulties facing various naturalist and conventionalist accounts might stem from a deeper and shared source: a metaphilosophical commitment to the idea that a good explanation should be reductivist and atomist. This section explains such assumption – and the less well-understood alternative.

What exactly are we asking a philosophical explanation of dignity and rights to do?

Here is an influential idea: the task of a philosophical explanation is reduction. And a reductivist explanation, as I'll understand it, has two features: atomistic decomposition and elimination. First, a reductivist philosophical explanation begins with a target notion (our explanandum), notices internal complexity, and then breaks it down into its component elements, seeking ultimately to reach simple, primitive, and unanalyzable elements (Strawson 1992: 17–18).[38] Second, a successful explanation is a form of elimination: unless the explanation is circular, the explanandum cannot be part of the explanans – and so must be, in a sense, eliminated.[39] For instance, you might construe David Hume's philosophical explanation of causation as the attempt to meet these two explanatory conditions. First, Hume decomposes what seems like a relational phenomenon (a nexus between cause and effect) into discrete,

---

[38] I'm grateful to Pablo Gilabert for alerting me to this discussion in Strawson's wonderful but somehow neglected treatise in metaphysics.

[39] For an excellent overview of reduction and fundamentality in metaphysics and philosophical explanations, see Marmodoro and Mayr (2019: 59–62).

non-relational, and simple occurring events. Second, Hume in a sense elimin-
ates the causal relation by explaining it in terms that make no reference to the
necessity of a causal nexus. Instead, the explanans is the succession in time of
discrete events.

However, reductivist explanations face two formidable difficulties. First, the
demand of decomposition runs into the difficulty that few, if any, explanans
really are utterly simple, primitive, and unanalyzable. What to one philosopher
will appear as utterly simple, primitive and unanalyzable (e.g., causes, beliefs,
normative reasons, duties) will appear to another as complex, derivative, and
ripe for analysis in some further terms. Second, the demand for reduction faces
a notorious dilemma. On the one hand, if the account succeeds in being non-
circular, the challenge is that it's unlikely to have secured *sufficient* conditions
for the explanandum. On the other hand, if the explanation succeeds in securing
sufficient conditions, then the challenge is that the explanation is likely to have
presupposed the very term that was supposed to be explained.

But if we give up the reductivist model, what's the alternative?

An alternative I find promising replaces reductivism with non-reductivism
and atomism for holism.[40]

In trying to capture the aims of a philosophical explanation, P.F. Strawson
once invited us to imagine

> the model of an elaborate network, a system, of connected items, concepts,
> such that the function of each item, each concept, could, from the philosoph-
> ical point of view, be properly understood only by grasping its connections
> with the others . . .. (Strawson 1992: 19)

Now in Jackson and Pettit's terms, we may call this model holistic or "networked." The model illuminates by making explicit connections among concepts and clarifying how these concepts form a network of ideas.

---

[40] A good example of a hybrid model might be the one propounded by Canberra realists like
Jackson and Pettit (1995) in the explanation of moral terms. Jackson and Pettit endorse what I'm
calling the "reductivist" dimension when they endorse the "supervenience" of the normative on
the non-normative – where "supervenience" is treated as a reductivist strategy. Interestingly,
Jackson and Pettit vigorously reject atomism: 'No simple atomistic definition is going to yield an
understanding of a moral term, because each such term is used in a way that presupposes a large
network of connections with other terms, evaluative and descriptive' (1995: 22). For excellent
examples of non-reductivist versions of supervenience about the normative, see Shafer-Landau
(2003: ch. 4) and Wedgwood (2007). As I see things, these two dimensions (reductivism and
holism) are in some tension with each other. If one admits that moral terms are 'networked', it
makes it even less likely that a successful reduction will be possible, since the normative terms in
question will make reference not just to other descriptive terms but to other *normative* terms; and
it's unlikely that a fully reductivist account could capture such interconnections. But for our
purposes here, I will only need the weaker claim that a presumption for a holistic and non-
reductive analysis stems from the difficulties a reductivist model has in explaining dignity and
rights – either naturalistically or conventionally.

But not *any* connection would do. What a networked explanation seeks is to demonstrate the *necessary* connections among *fundamental* concepts (Strawson 1992: 18–23). And a concept is *fundamental* in the sense that it is general and presupposed by other concepts – or, put more ontologically, a property is more fundamental when it doesn't depend on others but the others depend on it.

Notice that this notion of fundamentality involves the notion of irreducibility, but the notion of irreducibility is different from the familiar reductivist model. In the model of reductive analysis, a concept is irreducible in a *compositional* sense: x is irreducible$_{compositionally}$ if, and only if, x is utterly simple, containing no further, simpler elements. In the history of ethics, G.E. Moore once attempted to analyze the property of goodness this way, by treating "good" as an utterly simple, unanalyzable, and irreducible normative property (Moore 1903). By contrast, when we shift to the model of networked explanation, a concept is irreducible in a *fundamentality* sense: x is irreducible$_{fundamentally}$ if, and only if, it's a fundamental concept. For instance, to say that causation is irreducible in the fundamentality sense is to say that this concept or phenomenon cannot be eliminated without serious loss, for while it doesn't depend on other properties, many other properties or facts depend on it.

We can now clarify two important features of this notion of irreducibility. First, to say that x is irreducible$_{fundamentality}$ is *not* to say that x is utterly simple. For instance, Kant may have been correct in claiming that causation is an irreducible because fundamental category of theoretical thought without committing himself to the idea that causation is an utterly simple notion. And second, to say that x is irreducible$_{fundamentality}$ is *not* to say that x lacks any relations to other concepts. On the contrary, elucidating the nature of the concept may well require, as Strawson or Jackson and Pettit put it, showing how this concept fits into a network of *fundamental concepts*.

An important upshot of shifting from reductive and atomistic to non-reductivist and networked analysis is that the guiding philosophical question shifts. Instead of asking, "what are the simple properties that explain, in a non-circular way, dignity and rights?" we'd ask the very different question: "are dignity and rights fundamental concepts?" "What roles do these concepts play in the network?"

Before tackling this question, two important clarifications. First, shifting the guiding question also shifts the explanatory demands on the account. To put it bluntly, stop worrying about circularity. As Strawson argued, circularity is a great theoretical sin – but only if you presuppose the model of reductivist analysis.[41] By contrast, a non-reductivist, networked model of analysis may well lead to a view where fundamental concepts (such as causation and sub-stance; dignity and rights) are mutually dependent. If so, it would be impossible to understand one without the other, and the demand for non-circularity would be an obscuring hangover from the reductivist model. Second, a clarification of my argumentative scope. Naturally, I can't *prove* in what remains that dignity and rights are fundamental concepts. Instead, I'll begin to sketch why one might think that these are fundamental concepts by considering arguments leading to the opposite conclusion, namely, that the concepts of dignity or rights may be eliminated. And I'll show that these arguments are more problematic than philosophers have thought.

3.2 A Metaphysics of Kinds and Dispositions

So how should a networked analysis proceed?

This is the second main idea I want to introduce: drawing from a metaphysics of kinds and dispositions and transposing it to the normative domain can illuminate the structure of dignity and rights.

Perhaps influenced by the legacy of logical positivism, for much of the twentieth century a metaphysics of kinds and dispositions would have been a nonstarter among metaphysicians – never mind among moral and political philosophers aiming for philosophical accounts free of metaphysics. However, as the radical empiricism of the logical positivists loses its grip, over the past thirty years or so, metaphysicians have once again begun to take seriously a less empiricist metaphysics of kinds and dispositions.[42] The moment is ripe, I think, for exploring how such a metaphysics might help illuminate the nature of normative concepts, like dignity and rights.

Now, philosophers have been thinking about what I'll call the Kind-Dispositional model at least since Plato and Aristotle, and I can't stay faithful

---

[41] I've been deliberately fudging the formulation of the point semantically in terms of concepts with an ontological formulation in terms of properties and relations. The reason for this fudge is that I suspect that at this point in this discussion, it doesn't much matter whether we focus on fundamental *concepts* or fundamental *properties and relations*. Ralph Wedgwood puts the point nicely and more ontologically when he says that "real definitions [This version of the task of a philosophical explanation] do not have to be reductive or non-circular. This, then, is the proposal that I shall try to develop here: that constitutive accounts are in fact nothing other than real definitions or statements of essence" (2007: 140). If you prefer the more ontological formulation, then, my project is giving a non-reductivist account of the essence of dignity and rights.

[42] For two seminal book-length studies, see Mumford (1998) and Molnar (2003). For important collections exploring the nature of dispositions, see Armstrong, Martin, and Place (1996) and Marmodoro (2010).

to the history of this tradition. Instead, I want to extract some core concepts from this rich and varied tradition.

Start with the concept of a kind. What is a kind? There are all manner of kinds: pebbles, coins, tables, water, tigers, white pines, humans. The idea of a kind that interests me is the roughly neo-Aristotelian view, articulated for instance by Jonathan Lowe, that there is an internal conceptual connection between individuals and kinds: individuals are essentially individuals of a kind, and kinds are essentially kinds of individuals (Lowe 1989: 11, 163). Kinds offer criteria of identity for individuals.

So understood, kinds are characterized dispositionally, that is, by dispositional properties.[43] Dispositional properties contrast with categorical or occurrent ones, perhaps, like shape or size. While dispositional properties are developmental, shifting from a state of potentiality to one of actuality, occurrent properties are not developmental but static.

For instance, when you think of this bit of water here, sitting in your water bottle, you probably think about it in kind-dispositional terms. You might think: water hydrates me; water dissolves salt; water freezes below certain temperatures; water evaporates over other temperatures. These are all activities characteristic of water. Not all kinds of things have these characteristic activities. Pebbles, for instance, don't. You could ingest pebbles, but they don't hydrate you. You could throw salt on a pebble, but the pebble won't dissolve it. And so on.

In general, the concept of a disposition might be understood as comprising three key aspects.[44] First, *reality*.[45] I assume that dispositions are real and not reducible to purely non-dispositional or occurrent properties.[46] This also means that dispositions can exist even in potentiality, that is, when they have not yet manifested. Water has the dispositional property of solubility or of hydrating you even if the water in your water bottle is never mixed with salt or no one ever drinks it. Second, *directionality* and *actuality*. Dispositions are directed toward certain kinds of manifestations but not to others (Molnar 2003: 57). The

---

[43] Another aspect of kinds, as I'll understand them, is that they are not static entities or properties but structural processes of dispositional activities. For an introduction to process philosophy, see Rescher (2000).

[44] My account here follows the discussion in Marmodoro and Mayr (2019: 63–71).

[45] I'm grateful for conversation with Christian Pfeiffer on this aspect of dispositions.

[46] To be sure, this being philosophy, some philosophers have attempted to reduce the notion of a disposition to non-dispositional notions. Gilbert Ryle (2009) once attempted to do so by analyzing dispositional statements in terms of occurrent predicates structured in conditional statements. There are good reasons to think this reduction has failed, as Martin powerfully argues by thinking about finks and masks (2008: 12–33). See also Marmodoro and Mayr (2019: 72–3). For our purposes, the only claim we need is that dispositions are real rather than illusory, not the much stronger claim that no fundamental properties are occurrent.

manifestation of a disposition makes it *fully actual* – rather than merely potential. And third, *reciprocity*. Manifesting into the range activity often requires what Martin called "reciprocal disposition partners" (Martin 2008: 3). For instance, for the solubility of water to manifest, it needs, say, salt as a reciprocal disposition partner.

To see the interdependence of kinds and dispositions, consider a simple example. What would you say if you had to explain to someone how to play chess? Most likely, your explanation would include, perhaps, some occurrent properties: the shape of the board, the shape of the pieces. But describing the shapes of the pieces, even if necessary, is not enough. No one would understand what chess *is* unless they also understood what the pieces *do*. That's why, in explaining chess, even if you mention occurrent properties (say, "this piece here is the queen"), you'd also explain the kind and its dispositions ("a piece of this shape is *the* queen and it moves in all directions. What's a rook? It's a kind that moves horizontally and vertically any number of squares so long as its path is not blocked by another piece. And so on").

My point about a metaphysics of kinds and dispositions is analogous. The point is not that occurrent properties don't matter or are somehow illusory (though that may be!). Rather, the point is that in order to explain certain phenomena, just as in chess, we *must* appeal to kinds and their dispositions. Sure, you may explain the internal chemical structure of water as *H2O*, but you won't fully understand what water is until you also understand it as a kind with characteristic dispositions.

3.3 Transition to a Metaphysics of Morals

My suggestion is that we can begin to develop a non-reductivist, networked analysis of dignity and rights as distinctively *normative* kinds and dispositions. The model gives us an explanation of their role: dignity's role is to mark a fundamental form of value anchored in kinds; the role of rights is to function dispositionally by specifying and realizing through duties of recognition the requirements of dignity. The going in this section may get a little tough, but the upshot will be this: the metaphysical interdependence between kinds and dispositions transposes to the interdependence between dignity (as a kind-based value) and rights (as the deontic dispositions necessary to the kind directed to realization through recognition).

To begin to build a bridge from a metaphysics of kinds and dispositions to normative phenomena, consider Judy Thomson's idea that some kinds *are inherently normative*. She calls these *goodness fixing kinds*. Thomson's thesis:

> *Goodness-fixing Kinds*: *A* has the property of being good *qua K* if, and only if, *K* is a goodness-fixing kind. (2008: 20–1)

Goodness-fixing kinds fix normative properties by generating a normative ordering for members of the kind. For instance, our everyday statement "this is a good toaster" is analyzed in terms of the fact that an individual instantiates a goodness fixing kind. So, we may say that the kind toaster fixes facts about goodness such that individual toasters are better or worse depending on the extent to which the individual instantiates the characteristic dispositions of the kind: it toasts well, it doesn't burn bread; the artifact doesn't spontaneously combust; etc.

But what are goodness fixing kinds? The thought that some kinds might be inherently normative is suggestive but elusive. To render it more precise, consider what Michael Thompson calls "natural historical judgments" (2008: 64–7). These are judgments that attempt to explain normative properties in terms of the dispositions characteristic of certain kinds, namely, *living* kinds. Such judgments have the following form:

The *S* is/does *F*.

For instance, if we judge that the maple turns its leaves red in the fall, we can judge that this individual maple here, lacking leaves, does not fail to be a maple but fails to be as it *should* through weakness, disease, etc. An order of natural historical judgments representing the distinctive activities of the kind, then, enables us to ground normative judgments about what *individuals* should do, about the goodness of individual actions. Following Anscombe, Thompson calls a system of such judgments "Aristotelian categoricals" (2008: 66). In our terms, Aristotelian categoricals represent a Kind-Dispositional model for the explanation of living beings.

Though more informative than Judy Thomson's goodness-fixing kinds, Thompson's natural historical judgments need further specification.[47] What interests me is a thought that thinkers in this neo-Aristotelian tradition often miss, namely, a conceptual gap between Aristotelian categoricals and deontic notions like dignity and rights.

Grant that the goodness fixing kind, say, toaster or maple, fixes an evaluative ranking of normative standards. Such standards ground evaluative judgments *comparing* how well individual instances manifest the characteristic functions or dispositions of the kind. "The toaster applies moderate heat to slices of bread

---

[47] Philippa Foot (2001) has argued that Thompson's Aristotelian categoricals fail to distinguish statistical generalities from genuinely normative judgments (e.g., "the maple's leaves rustle in the wind" has the grammatical form of a natural historical judgment without grounding any normative judgment). I bracket this gap to focus on a second one.

without spontaneously starting a fire," say, grounds evaluative judgments comparing individual toasters. Following Gregory Vlastos's formulation, let's call this form of goodness *merit* (1984).

Note that merit is not just a property of artifacts like toasters. It's a general form of predication for any goodness fixing kinds grounding evaluative comparisons. We might say of this white pine that it's healthier than that one, or of this rational agent that it's more vicious than that. And so on.

But if this were the only fundamental form of predicating goodness, something fundamental would be missing.

As Gregory Vlastos argued, when we think about the value of individuals and how individuals matter, we are not evaluating their actions against some comparative evaluative standard. Instead, we are valuing *the individual as such*. And, as Vlastos noticed, the form of goodness involved here is fundamentally different, for it is not comparative and, I'd add, fundamentally deontic (i.e., connected to notions of obligations and rights). Vlastos called this form of goodness an individual's *worth*. We may as well call this form of goodness the individual's *dignity*.

So here's the proposal: think of dignity as a fundamental form of goodness characterizing the nature of a kind. Such form of goodness differs fundamentally from the comparative and evaluative form we may call *merit*. Their difference is functional: while merit plays the role of grounding comparative orders of evaluation, worth plays the role of grounding non-comparative deontic orders, the rights and obligations essential for realizing such value.

Indeed, with Kant, we can distinguish the goodness that obtains from *securing one's purposes* and the goodness that obtains *from being an end in itself.*

> The ends that a rational being proposes at his discretion as *effects* of his actions (material ends) are all only relative ... But suppose there were something the *existence of which in itself* has an absolute worth, something which as *an end in itself* could be a ground of determinate laws. (*G,* 4:428)

We can abstract from exegetical details to capture the following point: while the notion of merit attaches to the attainment of evaluative standards, there is a different form of fundamental goodness: the existence of a being as an end in itself.

This suggests that, following Vlastos, we can distinguish two forms of fundamental goodness:

> *Merit-fixing Kinds*: A has the property of being good *qua K* if, and only if, *K* is a goodness-fixing kind.

> *Worth-Fixing Kind*: *A* has the property of dignity if, and only if, (i) *A* is a member of kind *K,* and (ii) *K* is a worth-fixing kind.

Still, a legitimate worry is that analyzing dignity in terms of worth-fixing kinds doesn't tell us very much. What's a worth-fixing kind in the first place?

This is where a Kind-Dispositional model can begin to shine. In general, kind-based predication would be conceptually empty without being complemented by the distinctive *dispositions* of the kind. To understand the concept *water*, you might say, you must master a number of inferences about what water *does* in a variety of circumstances. The thought transfers to the kinds envisaged by Thompson and Foot. To understand the concept of a white pine or a tiger, you must master a network of dispositions characteristic of the kind, what white pines or tigers characteristically do in a variety of circumstances through their life. My suggestion is that when we shift to worth-fixing kinds a similar structure is preserved. Specification of the nature of a kind as a worth fixing kind would be empty without complement by the distinctive dispositions of the kind. It's just that the distinctive dispositions of worth-fixing kinds take the deontic shape of *rights*. Just like distinctive non-normative dispositions fill in the distinctive activities of the kind, so too rights –as normative dispositions – specify the distinctive forms of activities or ways of being treated of beings with dignity, that is, of worth-fixing kinds.

To elaborate the idea further, let's connect the Hohfeldian axiom of correlativity to the notion of goodness as worth to obtain the following equivalences:

1. *Worth-Fixing Kind*: *A* has the property of dignity if, and only if, (i) *A* is a member of kind *K,* and (ii) *K* is a worth-fixing kind.
2. *Normative Dispositions*: If *A* is a member of a worth-fixing kinds, then the *A* performs activities expressive and characteristic of the worth-fixing kind.
3. *Right-Fixing Kinds*: If *K* is a worth-fixing kind, then *A, qua* instance of *K,* has fundamental claim-rights to respect from any agent, *B,* who is capable of having duties with regard to the activities or ways of being characterized by 2.

The equivalence makes explicit the *networked* structure of these practical concepts. The model analyzes dignity as a kind-based concept, one capturing a distinctive form of fundamental goodness or value, the *worth of individuals* (rather than the merit of actions). But what the networked pattern of the analysis predicts is that we can't understand this concept in isolation, just like we can't understand the notion of a kind in isolation. Instead, just as the concept of a kind requires elucidation through distinctive dispositions, so too the concept of the worth of individuals requires articulation through rights as normative dispositions to activity or ways of being. Dignity and rights, it emerges, can't be understood independently of each other precisely because they are elements in an indissoluble network of practical concepts. More ontologically formulated, dignity and rights must each be mentioned in giving any account of the other, so that the two properties are essentially interdependent, without either of the two being reducible to or independent from the other.[48]

The non-reductivist and networked character of the Kind-Dispositional Model changes our understanding of these concepts.

Start with dignity. One of the aspects of dignity we wanted to understand was how dignity entails a stringent duty of respect. That entailment is now secured by understanding dignity as a *fundamentally deontic* form of goodness. Dignity is a form of *worth,* rather than *merit;* and worth is conceptually connected to rights. Holding in place the Hohfeldian axiom, this gives us a natural explanation of the connection between dignity and a duty of respect. Dignity entails a duty of respect because claim-rights entail duties, and dignity entails claim-rights.

A Kind-Dispositionalist Model effects a similar transformation in our concept of rights. Just as Philippa Foot and Michael Thompson speak of "Aristotelian Categoricals," we can think of rights as "deontic categoricals," insofar as rights give deontic structure to the dispositions to action and ways of being expressive of a being's dignity.

In the basic case, rights are not instruments for the promotion of some independently intelligible value – some aspect of your well being or the value of your autonomous choices (as Interest and Will can seem to argue). Rather, the primary function of rights is relational and dispositional. The function is dispositional in the sense that rights structure forms of activities or ways of being expressive of the worth of individuals. And just like many dispositions require dispositional partners for their realization, so too with rights as normative dispositions: they are directed both to forms of activities expressive of dignity and to the recognition of such activity by others. The form such recognition takes is the other's duty with regard to the right, preserving the correlativity of rights and duties upheld by Hohfeld. The primary function of rights, then, is to express the realization conditions of a fundamental form of goodness and to enable forms of action expressive of such goodness, thereby marking out a correlative set of duties.

3.4 A Kind-Dispositionalist Model of Dignity and Rights: Beyond Naturalism and Conventionalism

In this short Element, I can only provide a formal sketch of the model without going into substantive questions (e.g., who exactly instantiates a worth-fixing

---

[48] Here, I paraphrase a point of Ralph Wedgwood on the interdependence of the normative and the intentional (2007: 163).

kind? What specific rights do we have?). Accordingly, a full vindication of the model cannot be provided here.

Nevertheless, I now argue, an important advantage of the model is that it seems well placed to accommodate both the recognition and the normativity conditions for dignity and rights. The model does so by exploiting an analogy to non-normative kinds and dispositions. Just like non-normative dispositions are directed to manifestation, so too dignity and rights are directed to manifestation in distinctive forms of activity or ways of being and so to the recognition of others. The actual recognition of dignity and rights matters because it makes dignity and rights fully actual and real; yet, the account need not be conventionalist, since dignity and rights can exist prior to manifestation – and so independently of specific conventions.

Start with fundamental dignity. The Kind-Dispositional model lets us think of dignity as a kind-based disposition that is *inherently relational and developmental.*

The Kind-Dispositional model can preserve the naturalist idea that dignity is a normative property that exists independently of specific social conventions. If dignity is a *natural* worth-fixing kind, it doesn't depend on social facts.[49] Suppose that all rational agents or that all living beings qualify as Worth-Fixing Kinds. Then, dignity would be a normative property attached to the kind of agent – *rational agent, living being* – and so it would bind others independently of conventional obligations.

Though the model can preserve this important insight of naturalism, it also departs from standard naturalist views, which represent dignity as a static, inherent, and non-relational property. By contrast, the Kind-Dispositional model represents dignity as a dynamic, relational, and processual normative property. Although the Kind-Dispositional model says that dignity is a property that inheres in individuals in virtue of their Worth-Fixing Kinds (and so is independent of social conventions) dignity is fundamentally dynamic and relational. Just as other dispositional properties, dignity is *directed to* forms of activity or ways of being treated consistent with this unique form of goodness and so is *relational* by being essentially directed to *recognition*. In this sense, dignity takes as its reciprocal disposition partner agents who are capable of guiding their actions through norms. And so, dignity is realized, manifest or fully actualized when such agents *recognize* your dignity. Conversely, forms of

---

[49] One virtue of the model, I think, is that it leaves room for specification along conventionalist lines as well. If dignity were construed as a *purely social* worth-fixing kind, then the resulting account would be conventionalist. I leave this option conceptually open here but explore the naturalist version, which I personally find more promising.

misrecognition don't function as reciprocal disposition partners because they hinder the realization of dignity.

One way to frame the contrast to standard naturalist views might be as follows: while naturalist views *thingify* dignity, the Kind-Dispositional model represents dignity as a developmental process directed to recognition *by* others. And this difference enables us to see better than standard naturalist views why recognition matters: recognition matters because without it dignity can't be realized.

Put now as a contrast to conventionalist views, the Kind-Dispositional model can capture the significance of recognition without necessarily making dignity a socially contingent property. *If* dignity is anchored by a natural worth-fixing kind, such kind is inherently normative. As a result, the trilemma of normativity doesn't arise in the first place – since we're no longer trying to bridge the gap between purely social facts and normative ones.

In short, my argument is that already at this great level of generality, an important advantage of the Kind-Dispositional model is that it appears better able to meet the demands of recognition and of normativity than more familiar naturalist and conventionalist views.

We can repeat the same form of argument for a Kind-Dispositional account of natural rights. To see this, consider the following schema:

> *Natural Rights Schema*: R is a natural right just in case R is a necessary specification of a way of action or way of being for a Worth-Fixing Kind directed to recognition by others.

The Kind-Dispositional model suggests understanding natural rights as those fundamental rights that are necessary specifications of action or ways of being for a natural Worth-Fixing kind.[50] Articulating the nature of dignity and funda-mental rights requires a process of articulation for specific natural and social conditions. The parallel to Aristotelian categoricals might help here.

Foot puts the point by addressing the objection that facts about a species seem subject to change. Her response is that such Aristotelian categoricals "tell how a kind of plant or animal, considered at a particular time and in its natural habitat, develops, sustains itself . . ." (2001: 29). The same point holds for natural rights. The idea is *not* that if a right is natural then it's outside of history and not subject to change. On the contrary, natural rights are dynamic, for they specify for particular times and particular social habitats what dignity

---

[50] That they are specifications need not mean that they are mere means for the production of some independent value or that the rights are deduced through conceptual analysis of the value. For more detailed discussion, see Zylberman (2016b).

requires.[51] What makes natural rights *natural* is that their validity is independent of social *conventions,* not that they are outside of time or social space.

Having introduced the schema for natural rights, we can return to the contrast to the standard accounts.

With naturalist views, the Kind-Dispositional Model can understand some rights, fundamental ones, as existing independently of specific social conventions. For instance, say that you have fundamental rights to not be tortured, enslaved, or deceived. Or say that cows and chickens have fundamental rights not to be treated with cruelty. The Kind-Dispositional Model would understand such fundamental claim-rights as necessary normative properties attached to the Worth-Fixing Kind – *human being, sentient being* for specific contexts of action and interaction.

Fundamental rights are inherently relational, dynamic and processual normative properties attached to fundamental dignity. Much like specific dispositions articulate the nature of a kind, specific fundamental rights articulate the normative nature of dignity. They specify what the kind *does* in a normative sense. Humans have a way of being consistent with their dignity, say, when they are not tortured, deceived, or enslaved. Cows and chickens have a way of being consistent with their dignity, say, if they can live without cruelty by humans.

The primary function of rights, then, is to make socially possible ways of being or ways of acting consistent with the requirements of a Worth-Fixing Kind. Just like normative rules specify the nature of a kind in chess (e.g., what the queen is) and what the kind does (e.g., the queen's distinctive moves), so too rights are normative rules specifying what the Worth-Fixing Kind is and does. Rights differ from other normative rules in enabling forms of being or acting that are dispositionally directed to recognition *by* others. Such recognition by others takes the form of the other's *duty.* And when such duties are not observed, the specific right is violated, which is to say, that a way of being or acting is *hindered* from full manifestation or actualization in the social world.

Turn now to Rights Conventionalism. The central thesis of rights conventionalism is the denial that natural rights exist, since every right requires recognition by some social convention for its existence.[52] By contrast, the Kind-Dispositional model provides a schema for understanding Natural Rights and so can make conceptual space for natural rights.

There is presumptive warrant, then, to conclude that the Kind-Dispositional model has the resources to meet the demands of recognition and of normativity

---

[51] For a parallel vision in the Kantian tradition, see Herman (2021).

[52] See, again, Darby (2009: 1).

while avoiding some of the signature challenges affecting standard naturalist and conventionalist views.

Though I can't provide a fuller defense of the model here, I'd like to develop it further by testing it against three salient objections concerning (i) vicious circularity; (ii) extensional adequacy; and (iii) redundancy.

The first objection can be set aside quickly. As we saw earlier, circularity is a grave sin, as Strawson put it, for reductive analyses. If you are attempting to provide a reductivist explanation, the fact that the explanans contains a notion to be explained is a serious problem indeed. However, if you are attempting to provide a non-reductivist, networked analysis of these concepts, circularity is not a problem. The issue is whether the analysis can show the relevant concepts to be fundamental. For this reason, I'll focus on the second and third objections, which question the fundamental status of these concepts.

3.5 The Generality of the Model

To assess the generality of the model, let's run through the standard counter-examples to naturalist and conventionalist views. Again, my point is not to establish the extensional correctness of the model, but, more modestly, to explore some conceptual resources of the model for avoiding some of the standard counter-examples.

Before turning to specific cases, a general remark. What I take to be distinctive of the Kind-Dispositional model is its holistic and non-reductive explanatory structure. To the extent that the leading Interest and Will models seek to offer a reductive analysis, then the Kind-Dispositional model will stand opposed to them. And to the extent that these models make no reference to dignity, that's a second important contrast to the standard analyses. That said, it may be possible to develop non-reductivist and holistic variants of Interest or Will, in which case, the Kind-Dispositional model may indeed be *filled in* in either an Interest or Will direction. So, it's important to bear in mind that, from a strictly conceptual point of view, the models need not be opposed to each other. However, since the standard models typically are construed as offering reductive analyses of rights, in what follows I treat the models as contrastive rather than complementary.

So suppose that there is a natural right to property. According to Interest, necessary to the existence of such a right is that having property be typically beneficial to property owners. By contrast, according to the Kind-Dispositional model it is not a necessary condition of such a right that it be typically beneficial for property owners. As an empirical matter of fact, having property rights may make us worse off, say, by introducing social pathologies, such as inequality, oppression, or exploitation that wouldn't otherwise occur.[53] However, suppose that property rights were required specifications of dignity, such that part of their function was to enable forms of recognition of each other's equal dignity. The analysis could be filled in variously. A Lockean may insist that property rights function to enact freedom, insofar as property rights package moral powers that enable agents to have exclusive control over things (Simmons 1992: 72). Similarly, a Kantian could analyze property rights as packaging our relational freedom vis-à-vis one another when it comes to the use of non-persons (Ripstein 2009: ch. 4). A Marxist could argue that many forms of property are in fact not genuine natural rights precisely because such forms of property rights are inherently *inimical* to the social realization of dignity – perhaps, private property rights are necessarily alienating. The main lesson, I take it, is the following: *even if* it turned out that property rights were neither typically beneficial to humanity nor to individual property owners (see Kramer 2017: 71), Interest and the Kind-Dispositional model would yield different predictions. Interest would be committed to the absence of natural property rights. By contrast, the Kind-Dispositional model could accommodate them – so long as a plausible case could be made that such rights are necessary specifications of dignity. And so, *if* natural property rights could be construed as counter-examples to Interest, they need not be counter-examples to the Kind-Dispositional model.

The other large category of counter-examples to Interest is conventional rights that are not obviously connected to what is typically beneficial. I return to this category in the next section, when we extend the model to socially constituted rights.

But before moving on, let's pause to consider an important objection. A defender of standard Interest might grant the point about divergent analyses of natural property rights but insist that the Kind-Dispositional model fails when explaining other natural rights, such as to food or health, that necessarily appeal to aspects of our well-being. How can we understand such rights without appealing to aspects of well-being?[54] The issue is that if the Kind-Dispositional model can only specify such rights by appealing to interests, then the model collapses into Interest.

However, I think this important objection is, at bottom, based on a *non-sequitur*. It doesn't follow from the fact that an explanatory model appeals to interests that the model collapses into Interest. That's because there are two ways of understanding the role interests play in the theory. I've suggested that

---

[53] Wenar envisages a problem like this for Interest (2013: 205, fn. 9). Kramer provides a detailed response (2017: 70–2).

[54] I'm grateful to Rowan Cruft for pressing this worry.

the standard role interests play in rights theory is in filling in conditions for a reductivist and atomistic analysis. Nevertheless, interests can enter the theory differently: not as reductivist explanans, but as material aspects of the agency of Worth-Fixing kinds. Since such material aspects need not be properties that matter independently of deontic concepts, like dignity and rights, interests can indeed play a role in such a model – just not the standard reductivist role.

To illustrate, consider a right to food.[55] The Kind-Dispositional model can grant that if we were creatures without nutritional needs, it wouldn't be intelligible to assign us a fundamental right to food. But this concession entails no commitment to Interest (understood as a reductivist model). For one thing, the concession doesn't entail that the satisfaction of interests is a *necessary* condition of any rights – a core conceptual thesis of standard Interest. For another, aspects of well-being function differently in the model. A Kind-Dispositional model would specify the material conditions, the habitat, of the relevant kind and say that relational nutritional contexts provide the occasion for manifesting or hindering dignity. In contexts where people lack adequate access to food, they are vulnerable to hindrances to dignity, say, through humiliation, subordination, marginalization. And for children of our kind, lack of adequate access to food is not merely a detriment to their well-being, it's also a hindrance to their full realization as members of a kind and a hindrance to the full social manifestation of their dignity.[56]

Perhaps one way to put the contrast, then, is that the Kind-Dispositional model has a hylomorphic approach to well-being. This would mean that interests can appear in the specification of the content of some natural rights, but the significance of the interests in question is not fully intelligible independently of the deontic requirements of dignity. Rather, the deontic requirements of dignity come first and then the question is how such requirements are to be specified for creatures with fundamental interests like ourselves. So, whereas Interest (typically) follows the reductivist project of explaining deontic properties in terms of non-deontic evaluative properties, the Kind-Dispositional model never attempts such reduction. Instead, aspects of well-being are already "colored" or "structured," as it were, by the deontic demands of dignity.[57]

---

[55] In a very different context, Barbara Herman makes what I take to be a parallel point in offering a Kantian analysis of the right to housing (2021).

[56] I begin to develop such an approach to poverty in general in Zylberman (2023b).

[57] I think Pablo Gilabert makes the very same hylomorphic point about the relation between dignity and interests when he articulates the following, illuminating metaphor: 'Another way to put these points, suggested to me by James Nickel, is to introduce an "oak barrel" account of the concept of human dignity. Some concepts are used as containers carrying content that can fully be accounted for without using them. When that is the case, the concepts are like stainless steel barrels which do not affect the taste of what they carry. But sometimes barrel concepts operate as oak barrels which partly affect the content of what they carry. In the metaphor, the flavor of

Turn now to Will. Once again, the *typical* versions of Will are reductivist (by seeking necessary and sufficient conditions that make no reference to claim-rights) and atomist (by not appealing to dignity). But it remains conceptually possible, I think, to elaborate a version of the Kind-Dispositional model that is specified along lines similar to Will. That said, I proceed assuming the contrast between the two models rather than the complementary versions.

One of the thorns in the side of any version of Will[58] stems from beings who appear to have rights but lack any form of normative control: very young children, the comatose, some elderly people who are incapacitated, nonhuman animals. Since the Kind-Dispositional needn't make normative control a necessary condition of rights possession, it can, in principle, accommodate such cases.

To illustrate, return to Margo, the two-year-old we considered previously. Suppose Margo suffers from neglect and domestic abuse. Since Margo lacks any form of normative control, Will theorists appear committed to saying that Margo can't have any rights – and so, can't be wronged. But the Kind-Dispositional model can accommodate fundamental natural rights for very young human beings precisely because what bestows such individuals with rights is a metaphysical property, membership in a Worth-Fixing Kind. As a kind-based analysis, the model can attribute certain rights to individuals simply in virtue of membership in the kind, abstracting away from specific stages of development. For instance, if Worth-Fixing kinds for humans involves a natural right to life and physical integrity, there is no conceptual barrier to attributing such rights to Margo – even when Margo lacks any form of norma-tive control.

The same point can be made about cruelty to animals. Perhaps the correct, substantive specification of the Kind-Dispositional model is in a biocentric direction, where one would claim that any living being is a Worth-Fixing Kind. If so, we would be able to explain the cruelty of the farmers to the cows (as in Cruft's example previously) *directly* as a wrong to the cows themselves. The model can thus explain those rights directly without having to modify the theory to introduce normative control exercised *on behalf* of others.

In sum, in articulating the Kind-Dispositional model, I've bracketed substan-tive and extensional questions about dignity or rights. In this subsection, I've argued that the model has conceptual resources to handle some of the standard counter-examples to Interest and Will. Of course, whether the model is exten-sionally accurate must be left for further investigation. My only point was to

---

a wine that is stored in an oak barrel will change, while it would remain the same in a stainless steel barrel' (2019: 148).

[58] Or, for that matter, of hybrid accounts such as that offered by Sreenivasan (2005).

highlight the promising character of the model and the conceptual resources it can marshal to handle familiar difficulties. Another tantalizing possibility to explore in the future is non-reductive and holistic variants of Interest or Will that complement (rather than oppose) the Kind-Dispositional model.

3.6 Irreducibility?

The Kind-Dispositional Model supports the thesis that basic dignity and basic rights are irreducible. They are not irreducible in the decompositional sense that dignity and rights are utterly simple, unanalyzable concepts. Rather, they are irreducible in the sense that they are fundamental categories of practical thought – or, more ontologically, normative properties essential to certain kinds of beings. But is that so?

Many philosophers appear to think otherwise, supposing that the concepts of dignity and of rights are not fundamental.[59] Here, I can't show such a supposition is mistaken. But I want to sketch an argument to put pressure against it. The Kind-Dispositional Model generates a powerful Anti-Elimination argument: familiar attempts at elimination are either inconsistent (by continuing to presuppose the *eliminandum*) or just change the topic – but at a high theoretical cost.

The general challenge to the irreducibility of dignity and rights is that these concepts are not fundamental, since they can be eliminated without serious theoretical cost. There are various ways of making this point. For instance, Steven Pinker argues that dignity is a "stupid" concept.[60] Andrea Sangiovanni argues that we don't need dignity, since other notions such as moral inequality, cruelty, or suffering do the explanatory work (2017). Shelly Kagan claims that "pretty much everything that people normally want to say in the language of rights can be expressed in terms of other normative factors and distinctions" (Kagan 1998: 171). Margaret Gilbert claims moral theory will be largely "untouched" without claim-rights (Gilbert 2018: 289). And Rowan Cruft says that rights need make "no 'extensional' difference to what ought to happen" (Cruft 2019: 1). In addition, the philosophical literature seems to implicitly

---

[59] Recently, with increased interest in relational forms of normativity, many philosophers have taken more seriously the idea that the notion of rights may be a core notion in moral thought and talk. Excellent recent examples include Stephen Darwall (2006), R. Jay Wallace (2019), Jonas Vandieken (2019), and Kieran Setiya (2022). These views share many affinities to the one defended here, but perhaps the starkest contrast is my insistence that both notions of dignity and rights are interdependent. What's distinctive here is my defense of their interdependence via the Kind-Dispositional model. For an illuminating overview of "second-personal" approaches to moral obligation, see Schaab (2023).

[60] Pinker (2008). For critical discussion of Pinker's skeptical critique, see Beitz (2013) and Bird (2021: 12, 28–30).

support this elimination by the fact that theorists of dignity rarely appeal to rights, and theorists of rights rarely appeal to dignity. In short, all these philosophers may have different things in mind when they suggest that the notions of dignity or of claim-rights can be eliminated. However, they appear to share the basic thought that dignity and rights, contrary to what I've suggested, simply are not fundamental and irreducible.

In response, I articulate the following *Anti-Elimination Argument.*

A. *Dignity-Rights Nexus*: There is a conceptual connection between natural rights and a fundamental form of goodness (the worth or dignity of individuals).[61]
B. Given the *Correlativity Axiom*, the elimination of natural claim-rights entails the elimination of duties of respect owed to individuals.
C. *Recognition Respect*: But if individual *A* is an instance of a Worth-Fixing Kind, then recognition respect of *A* is a necessary way to register *A*'s worth.

> *Conclusion*: Therefore, if you eliminate dignity and/or natural rights, you can't make sense of a fundamental form of goodness (dignity) and the basic duties of recognition respect attached to such good.

Here's a brief explanation of the argument. A is a conclusion from the earlier 1–4 argument, making explicit a conceptual connection between the notions of fundamental dignity and rights. The idea was that dignity is a distinct form of goodness precisely because its non-instrumental and non-comparative character is explained by its deontic structure, that is, its being constituted by rights. Viewed from the other side, natural rights enable forms of action and interaction that realize dignity. Premise B states the Hohfeldian Correlativity Axiom, which is widely held among philosophers of rights. So the key question is whether premise C is true.

The Kind-Dispositionalist model supports the truth of C as follows. As Stephen Darwall has famously argued, we should distinguish at least two notions of respect (1977, 2006). *Appraisal* respect is the fitting response to what I've called *merit*: the comparative value of some performance. To respect in this sense is to positively appraise the merit, say, of a soccer player in a World Cup final, or of a particularly beautiful chef's knife. By contrast, *Recognition respect* tracks what I've called *worth* or *dignity*. Moreover, this form of respect is conceptually tied to the *directed duties* constitutively correlated with claim-rights. The respect generated by dignity is *directed*, owed to the individual bearer of dignity. So C asserts, in effect, the equivalences I've been articulating.

---

[61] I provide a fuller account of this premise and so of the structure of ethical theory in Zylberman (2025).

Take out dignity or rights and you also make it impossible to make sense of the duty of respect we owe one another.

To further elaborate the Anti-Elimination let me draw out a corollary, the No Wrongs Argument.

D. *Wrongs*: The very concept of wronging someone presupposes that wrong-doer is violating a directed duty owed to victim.

> *Conclusion*: *No Wrongs*. In a world without dignity and rights, it's impossible to wrong one another.

Earlier I explained why many philosophers take D to be true, since there appears to be a conceptual connection between wrongs as a violation of a norm and the norm in question being directed to the wronged party. However, given B, the Correlativity Axiom, B and D together entail the No Wrongs conclusion. If you eliminate the claim-rights constitutive of dignity, it's impossible to wrong one another.

What begins to come into focus is a powerful argument in support of the fundamentality of basic dignity and rights. On the one hand, basic dignity and rights are fundamental precisely because they are respectively a fundamental form of goodness (dignity) and the deontic structure necessary to such goodness (rights). The upshot is that if you take away this form of value or rights, then it becomes impossible to make sense of the most basic forms of recognition respect we owe one another. On the other hand, given D Wrongs, it also follows that a world without dignity or rights is a world where individuals can't wrong one another in familiar ways. For instance, if *A* tortures, enslaves, or deceives *B*, then *A* may well do something wrong, but can't wrong *B*, since the very concept of a wrong presupposes *A*'s duties to *B*, or, equivalently, *B*'s claims against *A*.

Put together, the Anti-Elimination and the No Wrongs argument not only support the thesis that basic dignity and rights are fundamental concepts, they also put tremendous pressure against attempts at elimination. What they show is that such attempts will be ultimately inconsistent (by presupposing one of the key notions that was supposed to be eliminated) or, if consistent, the theoretical cost would be higher than many would be willing to shoulder. That's because if the interdependencies I've elucidated here hold, a world without dignity is also a world without natural rights or wrongs. Our language depicting such a world may not be inconsistent, but it would be radically impoverished.

First, if the *Anti-Elimination Argument* is sound, it shows that dignity is not a stupid concept, for it articulates a fundamental form of goodness that is not reducible to other forms of value. Dignity skeptics like Pinker appear to assume that we can eliminate dignity and still make sense of the notion of respect for persons, say, for their autonomy, or their moral status as beings who can suffer. But this assumption is mistaken. In order to hold fast to the relevant form of respect as recognition for the value of the person, you need the correlative notion of respect – otherwise recognition respect collapses into appraisal.

Sangiovanni provides a more sophisticated elimination argument. Though Sangiovanni seeks to eliminate the notion of dignity, he remains committed to the idea of equal status, respect, and rights:

> equal moral status is constituted by or consists in a bundle of rights against certain kinds of inferiorizing treatment (rather than the other way around), and, second, our commitment to moral equality is explained by or grounded in the rejection of inferiorizing treatment as socially cruel (rather than the other way around). (2017: 103)

Sangiovanni appears to offer a reductivist explanation:[62] moral equality and rights are moral facts grounded in the independently intelligible badness of social cruelty. But does such reduction work?

There's good reason to remain skeptical. First, Sangiovanni preserves the conceptual connection between moral status and rights. Second, to make sense of that connection, Sangiovanni appeals to the disvalue of social cruelty. However, there are two ways of thinking about this value.[63] Either it's a form of demerit, or it's a misrecognition of worth. And with either option, the attempted elimination fails.

Suppose the form of disvalue is a kind of *demerit,* a failure to appreciate the merits of another's actions. If so, then social cruelty becomes conceptually detached from equal status and rights. It becomes possible to be cruel to *x* without necessarily violating *x*'s rights or status. Perhaps you can be cruel to a cat or a tree without that entailing the concept that you've violated the cat or the tree's claim-rights. But if so, cruelty as such doesn't suffice for the deontic ideas of status and rights.

Alternatively, suppose the disvalue of social cruelty involves what I've called a misrecognition of worth. Perhaps, Sangiovanni can say that the distinctive mark of *social* cruelty – as opposed to the cruelty you might express in harming cats or destroying trees for fun – is precisely that it misrecognizes the status of your addressee. If this is the line taken, I grant that the notion of *social* cruelty is

---

[62] Commitment to the model of reductivist analysis appears to be manifested by Sangiovanni's insistence on directions of priority and explanation. If Sangiovanni's account is not reductivist, then rights and status are not eliminated. And if they are not eliminated, since they themselves entail commitment to dignity as I've understood it, Sangiovanni doesn't provide an elimination argument after all. So, in what follows, I assume that Sangiovanni can eliminate dignity precisely by attempting to provide a reductivist analysis.

[63] There might be a third, but if so, Sangiovanni doesn't explain it – to my knowledge.

rich enough to be sufficient for status and rights. But then the problem is that what makes *social* cruelty distinct is precisely that the notion *presupposes* the deontic concepts of the rights and the worth of individuals it had sought to eliminate.

Disambiguating the notion of cruelty exposes a weakness in Sangiovanni's elimination argument. If the notion of cruelty is thin enough, then the notion is not sufficient to explain rights or equal status. But if the notion of cruelty is thick enough to capture recognition respect, then the notion already presupposes the correlative deontic ideas of rights and dignity. Either way, the elimination appears to fail.

The same structural problem affects attempts to eliminate rights. Suppose we took Kagan's proposal to its extreme and eliminated all the notions I've been suggesting co-entail each other: dignity, rights, and recognition respect. Imagine a world where the only thing that matters is the promotion of the impersonal and intrinsic value of pleasure. Then the elimination attempt may not fail by being ultimately incoherent, but it would fail by imposing an extremely high theoretical cost.

This is where the No Wrongs argument becomes salient. A world without rights is a world without dignity and recognition respect. Fine, Kagan might say. But the key corollary is that this would also be a world where it's *impossible* to wrong one another. Torture, deceit, slavery all may be bad in various ways to the extent, say, that they produce suffering. But a fundamental normative property would be lost: in torturing, deceiving, enslaving one another, we can do one another no wrong.

The failure of reduction here is not due to inconsistency, but to implausibility. It rings false to say, paraphrasing Kagan, that we can capture most of what people want to say in the language of rights in a language that has eliminated rights. For one thing, I've argued that we wouldn't have space for the distinct and fundamental form of goodness characterizing dignity. Recognition respect would be unintelligible. For another, we would be unable to wrong one another. Purged of these concepts, the language need not be inconsistent, but it would be unrecognizable and would certainly not capture most of what people want to say when they reach for the language of rights.

In sum, many philosophers think that the concepts of dignity and/or rights can be eliminated without serious loss. To such philosophers, my claim that dignity and rights are fundamental will seem obviously false. I can't show these philosophers are mistaken. Still, I think the Anti-Elimination argument coupled with the No Wrongs argument put considerable pressure against the eliminativist view. It may well be that such elimination is in principle coherent, but

I think these arguments show that bereft of the concepts of dignity and rights, our moral thought and talk would be profoundly impoverished.

4 Conventional Rights: A Kind-Dispositional Model

While the previous section focused on a Kind-Dispositional model of natural rights, the current one sketches the model for non-natural or conventional rights. A full specification of the model is not feasible here. Instead, my aim is to show that the Kind-Dispositional model fits particularly nicely with what metaphysicians call the "Standard Model of Social Ontology." Then, I contrast this model with the Kind-Desire model recently advanced by Leif Wenar. Instead of focusing on the extensional accuracy of Wenar's model, as others have done (e.g., Kramer 2017 or May 2017), I focus on the reductivist structure of the account and press the same dilemma I've been pressing on other reductivist analyses of rights.

4.1 Transition from a Natural to a Social Metaphysics of Kinds

If dignity and rights are understood dispositionally, then the fact that they are directed to recognition means that the completion of their reality calls for the institution of social kinds. Such social kinds resolve a problem of metaphysical indeterminacy and thus enable distinct forms of action and agency.

As we've seen, when it comes to the question of the relation between natural rights and social conventions, philosophers typically follow two broad traditions. On the one hand, what I've called the naturalist tradition articulates a view perhaps represented by John Locke. Natural rights are inherent, non-relational properties of individuals, and we need social conventions, like the state, for instrumental reasons: to better protect independently intelligible rights (Simmons 1992). On the other hand, according to conventionalist views, such as that of Thomas Hobbes, Jeremy Bentham, and to some extent David Hume, social conventions are fully constitutive of rights: rights are the byproduct of conventions. Still, the social conventions are not arbitrary but are put in place for a reason: to produce better outcomes, such as greater aggregate well-being or better compliance with the standpoint of an impartial yet benevolent spectator.[64]

Though these traditions can appear conceptually exhaustive and mutually exclusive, in the previous section I argued that the Kind-Dispositional Model offers a genuine alternative to these broadly empiricist views. Not only are dignity and rights elucidated in a non-reductive way, but they are also

---

[64] For excellent discussion of David Hume on natural and artificial virtues, see Cohon (2006).

understood as inherently developmental, processual, and relational properties. Recognition literally completes the reality of basic dignity and rights. While the previous section focused on natural rights and fundamental dignity, let's turn now to the social dimension of dignity and rights.

On the Kind-Dispositional Model, then, social kinds are necessary not for Lockean or Humean instrumental reasons. Basic dignity and fundamental rights are neither fully determinate, inherent, and non-relational properties (as the Lockean naturalist claims), nor are they fully constituted by conventions (as the Hobbesian conventionalist claims). Rather, social kinds are a key stage in the development and completion of metaphysically indeterminate pre-conventional dignity and rights.[65] Since dignity and rights are directed towards completion through recognition, truly completing this process requires the establishment of social kinds to specify and render less metaphysically indeterminate the abstract and general properties of dignity and natural rights.

One way to get at the problem is through the complaint that basic dignity and rights are too vague, empty, and indeterminate.[66] For example, Michael Rosen discusses a legal case brought by M. Manuel Wackenheim against the commune of *Morsang-sur-Orge*. In 1991, the commune had passed a law banning the practice of "dwarf-tossing," a practice where little persons, such as M. Wackenheim, are thrown by competitors into the air, landing on an airbed. The mayor's rationale for the ban was that such form of entertainment represented a "violation of respect for the dignity of the human person" (Rosen 2012: 64). In opposition, Wackenheim argued that it was the *legal prohibition* itself that violated his dignity, by blocking him from exercising a form of employment of his own choice. The lesson Rosen draws from this case is that "the ubiquity of dignity in current legal discourse masks a great deal of disagreement and sheer confusion" (Rosen 2012: 67).

There is a sense in which Rosen is exactly right. The legal saga involving Wackenheim is plagued by a stubborn confusion between what I called

---

[65] In articulating this thought, I draw inspiration from the Kantian tradition. On one way of understanding this tradition, natural rights are 'provisionally' valid because in a state of nature such rights are inherently unstable, requiring *conceptual* completion through the institutions of a public authority (Ripstein 2009; Hasan 2018; Herman 2021; Stone and Hasan 2022). For competing readings see (Pippin 2006; Hodgson 2010; Pallikkathayil 2010, 2017; Ebels-Duggan 2012). Abstracting away from exegetical disagreements, the thought I'd like to extract from this tradition and then generalize is the following: if one understands the basic nature of dignity and rights dispositionally, then such properties require actualization through established forms of social recognition. Just as a public authority is required for the conceptual completion of natural right concepts, I'm suggesting, natural rights and fundamental dignity require *metaphysical* completion through established, social forms of recognition – including, but not limited to, public law.

[66] For illuminating discussion of this line of objection, see Gilabert (2018: §6.1). As exponents of this objection, Gilabert (2018: 142) mentions Orend (2002: 87–9) and Rosen (2013: 143–7).

fundamental and acquired dignity (recall the difference between comporting oneself *with* dignity and having basic status dignity). But even after introducing this bit of conceptual tidiness, a deeper problem remains. Is the practice of "dwarf-tossing" consistent with the basic dignity of Wackenheim or not? And what if Wackenheim is a voluntary participant of the practice? A can of worms has just been opened. Does basic dignity support or prohibit public health care, public employment insurance, or prostitution?

That the language of dignity can be used to support both sides of heated moralized arguments is taken as evidence by skeptics that dignity is a useless because too indeterminate concept.

However, notice that the skeptical form of reasoning here rests on the following dilemma. Either dignity is a useful practical concept – in which case basic dignity generates perfectly determinate requirements on action and basic rights – or, conversely, if the requirements on action are not perfectly determinate and the rights not fully specified, then the concept is too vague to be of any use.

Yet, this may be false dichotomy.

That fundamental practical concepts are metaphysically indeterminate doesn't mean that these concepts are faulty or useless. In fact, their very indeterminacy is a necessary feature of their function as perfectly general and abstract categories of practical thought. The Kind-Dispositional Model explains basic dignity and rights as processual properties that require completion and development through forms of interpersonal and social recognition. Indeed, in and of themselves the categories can sometimes remain too general, abstract, and vague, requiring more specific articulation and specification through social norms.

Yet, this concession doesn't mean that basic dignity and natural rights are totally empty or meaningless categories. Pablo Gilabert puts the point nicely:

> human dignity marks a distinctive kind of normative practice that focuses on what people owe to each other as human beings rather than as members of some class, race, or nation. (2019: 142)

Although basic dignity and natural rights can be metaphysically indeterminate, they are not totally empty, for they prohibit forms of action and interaction that attribute to some members of the kind a superior basic standing, a non-general suite of basic rights. Nevertheless, the problem of metaphysical indeterminacy remains. And its solution, I suggest, is not just *conceptual* specification of the requirements of dignity and rights, but *ontological* specification through social kinds. Social kinds are required, then, to complete the reality of basic dignity and rights and make them fully actual. To begin to elucidate the thought, let's turn to recent work in social ontology.

4.2 What Are Social Kinds? The Standard Model

I would now like to suggest that what metaphysicians call the "Standard Model of Social Ontology" provides a powerful elucidation of the notion of a social kind. But the Standard Model takes for granted, without explaining, the notion of a claim-right. I argue that the Kind-Dispositional Model has a particularly good fit with the Standard Model.

The "Standard Model of Social Ontology," as exemplified by John Searle (2010) or Kirk Ludwig (2017), conceptually links the notion of a social kind to rights, attributing to rights the function of enabling distinctive forms of activity. Let's start to unpack the model.

Searle begins with the key concept of a "status function":

> The distinctive feature of human social reality ... is that humans have the capacity to impose functions on objects and people where the objects and people [ii] cannot perform the functions solely in virtue of their physical structure. The performance of the function [iii] requires that there be a collectively recognized status that the person or object has, and [i]it is only in virtue of that status that the person or object can perform the function in question. (2010: 7)

In elucidating the notion of a status function, Searle highlights three aspects of social reality.

First, the notion of a status is not (just) the notion of some independent value. A status function is connected to a form of agency and to the dispositions characteristic of the social kind.

Second, status functions are not reducible to purely physical (or otherwise natural) properties. A twenty-dollar bill can't perform its status function – say, as means of exchange at a certain economic value – solely in virtue of its physical structure. To be sure, the physical structure matters, for instance, by helping us distinguish the real from the counterfeit bill. So the point is not that social reality transports us to an ontologically separate realm, a sort of Platonic heaven, or a domain of Cartesian immaterial substances. Rather, the point is that even when social reality is anchored in specific forms of material reality, the physical properties of the material object are not sufficient to ground the status functions. Why not?

The reason stems from a third feature of status functions: they are constituted by forms of social recognition.[67] Agents can perform the status function of

---

[67] For more detailed and illuminating discussion of this point, see Ludwig (2017: 111).

officiant at a wedding, police officer, or college professor not merely in virtue of their physical properties, but also in virtue of the requisite social recognition. The fact that you are amazing at directing traffic doesn't entail that you have the authority to do so, which is typically the exclusive purview of individuals socially recognized as police officers.

So, status functions enable distinctive forms of activities that are not explainable simply in virtue of purely physical properties precisely because social recognition of such status functions is also necessary.

With this sketch in place, let's focus now on a core feature of the Standard Model: the model analyzes status functions in terms of rights – but metaphysicians using this model rarely, if ever, explain the notion of a right. The Kind-Dispositional Model, I now suggest, can help to fill out that lacuna.

Searle suggests that status functions, "without exception . . . carry what I call 'deontic powers'"(2010: 8), rights, duties, obligations, permissions, entitlements. Similarly, Kirk Ludwig argues that the notion of a status role is necessarily connected with rights and obligations.

> Rights are held with respect to other holders of various status roles, and correspond to obligations on their part to not hinder or to facilitate, as their role requires, the exercise of the right. (Ludwig 2017: 143)

The important point for our purpose, then, is that the very notion of a right is necessarily connected to status functions and that rights play a crucial role in constituting the function. The primary function of the right is to enable a form of activity and, correlatively, to generate on others obligations not to hinder or to facilitate such activity. But if claim-rights constitute status functions, they also constitute social kinds. The connection between claim-rights and social kinds, it emerges, is constitutive rather than contingent or accidental. Another way to put this point is that if you abstract away from the notion of a claim-right, the very idea of a status function and of a social kind disappears from view.

To illustrate, when the DMV (at least in NY State) issues a D-Class license to you, it makes you

Eligible to drive:

- Passenger cars and trucks with a Gross Vehicle Weight Rating (GVWR) of 26,000 lbs. or less.
- Limited use motorcycles (mopeds).[68]

How should we analyze the social fact that you now possess a D-Class license? The Standard Model would provide the following analysis. First, having

---

[68] https://dmv.ny.gov/driver-license/nys-driver-license-classes.

a D-Class license is a status function constitutive of the social kind, *Operator* (that's the term used by DMV). The status comes packaged with activities you are now socially enabled to perform, such as driving passenger cars or mopeds, while ruling out other activities that you are *not* able to perform, such as any other kind of motorcycle, for which a different social kind is necessary. The status function, then, demarcates what we might call a "deontic sphere of agency," activities that you may or may not perform. As Ludwig puts it, the status function has a deontic structure in the sense that, as it confers rights on the possessor, it correlatively sets up obligations on others. This might be too obvious, but the state and your fellow citizens now have duties to not hinder you in functioning as an operator (say, by blocking you entrance to your own vehicle) and duties to facilitate this (say, by instituting a system of traffic rules where all can act as operators). Second, your being an instance of the social kind *D-Class Driver* is not a property you possess simply in virtue of your physical properties. Other individuals may in fact be better drivers than you, but if they live in a different jurisdiction, say, Australia, then they would lack the relevant social kind. And this brings out the third feature of social kinds: precisely because physical or natural properties are not sufficient to ground social kinds (they don't automatically make you a D-Class Driver), social forms of recognition are necessary. Yet, throughout, it's key to note that the status functions constitutive of the social kind *D-Class Driver* are *constituted by rights*.

Although I can't fully develop the argument here, at least on a first pass it can seem as if the Kind-Dispositional model fits better with the Standard Model than Interest and Will. To be sure, both Interest and Will can accommodate conventional or social rights. What's less clear is whether they have as good fit with the Standard Model as the Kind-Dispositional model. So let's examine that.

One difficulty for Interest is that, as Kramer puts it, a necessary condition of having a claim-right (even a conventional one) is that said claim-right must be typically beneficial for beings like the right-holder (Kramer 2017). However, it's not clear that the social kinds captured by the Standard Model are typically beneficial for their bearers.

For instance, imagine a social world where people are normally better off not having the status of drivers at all and are bound to move around either in non-polluting bicycles or in exclusively public means of transportation. But the fact that the D-Class status and the rights constitutive of it are so disconnected from your interests as an individual or our interests as humans shouldn't conceptually rule out the possibility of these rights. But that appears to be the prediction Interest would make: since a necessary condition is missing (possessing the status is not typically beneficial to the holder), then, contrary to what the Standard Model would say, the status *cannot* be constituted by claim-rights.

To be sure, Interest theories can finesse the analysis here, but at least on a first pass cases like these may show a poor fit between Interest and the Standard Model.

Similarly, Will appears to have a poor fit with the social kinds explained by the Standard Model because not all the rights constitutive of social kinds require normative control – however specified. The social kind soccer goalie, to use Wenar's example (2013), may come packaged with certain rights (e.g., against obstruction by opponent players) even if goalies lack normative control over such duties. Similarly, your status as a D-Class driver may come packaged with claim-rights against the drunk-driving collisions of others – even if you lack normative control over such duties.

By contrast, the Kind-Dispositional Model and the Standard Model appear to mutually illuminate and support one another. Here's the basic idea. The Kind-Dispositional model can make explicit the conceptual interdependence between normative kinds and claim-rights as the normative dispositional properties of the kind. The Standard Model, in turn, can fill in the model with socially concrete specifications of the kind and dispositions. The natural worth-fixing kind becomes specified as a concrete way of having worth as an individual, say, as a social kind: a citizen, a teacher, doctor, neighbor, driver, and so on. And the normative dispositions of the natural kind become socially concrete specifications of rights constitutive of the social normative status. Let me now try to elaborate on how these two models mutually illuminate and support each other.

To sharpen the Standard Model (and clarify what rights are necessary for social kinds), start with Sally Haslanger's important distinction between kind *K* having social causes and *K* being constituted socially. For instance, we might say, global warming has social causes but is not a social kind. By contrast, being a husband counts as a social kind not because having this status has social causes but because being a man legally married to another individual *constitutes* one as a husband (2003: 217). To capture this distinction, Haslanger proposes:

> *X is socially constructed constitutively as an F* iff *x* is of a kind or sort *F* such that in defining what it is to be *F* we must make reference to social factors (or: such that in order for *x* to be *F, x* must exist within a social matrix that constitutes *Fs*). (2003: 217)

I think this elucidation of the notion of a kind succeeds in contrasting the category of a social kind in opposition to faux-social categories, like global warming. However, it still seems too broad, because it doesn't let us distinguish what we may call *personal* social kinds (husband, woman, professor, class D driver) from *impersonal* social kinds (a twenty-dollar bill, a piece of property, a university).

The distinction between personal and impersonal social kinds matters because only personal social kinds are *directly* connected with rights. I think Searle and Ludwig are correct in making explicit a conceptual connection between social kinds and rights. But it also seems to me that impersonal social kinds (twenty-dollar bills or bits of property) are connected to rights derivatively, that is, through the personal kinds that are connected to them. Technically, it's not the bit of property that has rights, but the owner.

To capture the notion of a personal social kind, let's amend Haslanger's formulation, perhaps, as follows:

> *X is a personal social kind K* if, and only if, *K* is such that in defining what it is to be a *K* we must make reference to (i) social factors and (ii) to the rights constitutive of *K*.

This formulation helps to make explicit the direct connection some social kinds have to rights, namely, personal social kinds. To be an instance of the kind professor, mother, driver, citizen, or employee is for one to inhabit a kind that necessarily makes reference to (i) social factors and (ii) to the rights and deontic incidents constitutive of the kind. By contrast, impersonal social kinds – like currencies or bits of property – necessarily make reference to social factors but make *indirect* reference to rights. For instance, we can think of the concept of a dollar or the euro without making reference to an instance of the kind having rights. And when we steal something, we don't think we've wronged the stolen *item*, but that we've violated the property rights of the *owner.*

If social ontologists like Searle and Ludwig are correct in finding a conceptual connection between social kinds and rights, then this is an important lesson for rights theory – even if it is one that social ontologists or rights theorists themselves have not developed.

With the notion of a personal social kind in place, we are now ready to return to my main line of argument. Basic dignity and natural rights are, as skeptics often point out, metaphysically indeterminate categories. Though indeterminate, they are not completely empty. Yet, since the Kind-Dispositional model understands the connection between dignity, rights, and recognition as one of gradual completion and realization, the solution to the problem of indeterminacy is social recognition through social kinds. Social kinds solve the problem of metaphysical indeterminacy by constituting more concrete and socially actual forms of agency that encode the requirements of basic dignity and rights.

To see this point, consider the social kind *citizen of Nigeria.* Conventions exist for delineating the general nature of the social kind. For instance, in the 1955 *Nottebohm* case, the International Court of Justice said that

[a]ccording to the practice of States, to arbitral and judicial decisions and to the opinion of writers, nationality is a legal bond having as its basis a social fact of attachment, a genuine connection of existence, interest and sentiments, together with the existence of reciprocal rights and duties.[69]

Two features of this conception of nationality or citizenship are noteworthy. First, citizenship constitutes a particular type of social kind, a "legal bond," the recognition of a status under a given set of laws. Second, citizenship, as personal social kinds in general, is constituted by a suite of "reciprocal rights and duties." When you are or become a citizen of Nigeria, the social kind specifies your basic dignity and your basic rights. On the side of dignity, it makes the requirements of dignity more specific by conferring on you a status under a particular legal jurisdiction. But that status is packaged with a suite of rights, which, in turn, also play the metaphysical function of rendering more determinate the nature and requirements of your basic dignity and rights.

Before moving on, I should flag an issue that requires detailed elaboration elsewhere. If I'm correct in thinking that the Kind-Dispositional Model has a particularly good fit to the Standard Model, it's still important to bear in mind that *social kinds are double-edged swords*. Many social kinds will indeed be required for emancipatory purposes, that is, for the social actualization of dignity and natural rights. Citizenship may be a good example. That said, the model also predicts what many critical race and feminist theorists have been saying for a long time: many social kinds enable forms of activity that are not only inimical to basic dignity and rights, they also entrench and constitute social patterns of oppression. I think that's exactly right and that the Kind-Dispositional model can help illuminate structures of oppression by showing how certain social kinds are oppressive precisely by (i) contravening the natural norms specified by fundamental dignity and natural rights and by (ii) masking such forms of oppression through the vehicles of personal social kinds. Such social kinds are socially real but normatively illusory, masking "illusions of worth and entitlement," as I'd put it. But elaboration of this important line of thought must be left for another occasion.

Let's take stock. Familiar empiricist philosophical accounts tend to represent conventions in an instrumental way: either conventions recognize independently intelligible and fully determinate rights (Locke), *or* conventions fully create rights and status (Hobbes, Bentham, Hume) – but do so for some further value intelligible independently of dignity and rights. By contrast, the

---

[69] *Liechtenstein v. Guatemala* ICJ Reports, 1955, p. 23. Liechtenstein sought a ruling that Guatemala should recognize Friedrich Nottebohm as a Liechtenstein national. See also Carol A Batchelor, "Statelessness and the Problem of Resolving Nationality Status," *International Journal of Refugee Law*, Vol. 10, No. 1/2, 1998, pp. 159–60. Quoted in Manby (2016: ix).

Kind-Dispositional Model extracts a key thought from the Kantian tradition that opens up an alternative. Just as in the Kantian tradition the social institutions of the state are non-instrumentally required for the social realization of innate, natural rights, so too, and more generally, I've suggested that social kinds are required for the full realization and actualization of dignity and natural rights. Not only does the Kind-Dispositional model open up a path that helps us move beyond the impasse between naturalism and conventionalism, it also offers an analysis that has a particularly good fit with the influential Standard Model of Social Ontology.

4.3 Why Not Reductivism? The Kind-Dispositional versus Kind-Desire Models

To elaborate further the Kind-Dispositional model I'd like to contrast it with the superficially similar "Kind-Desire" model recently proposed by Leif Wenar. Wenar argues that the Kind-Desire model preserves the reductivist ambitions of Interest and Will analyses while avoiding all their standard counterexamples. The line of objection I'll raise does not turn mainly on extensional correctness[70] but focuses, instead, on an issue less central to the literature: the reductivist structure of the account.[71] I argue that the reductivist structure of the Kind-Desire Model makes it vulnerable to familiar difficulties of reductivist explanations in general: either the account fails to provide non-circular *sufficient* conditions, or, when the conditions appear to be sufficient, it's only because they are circular.

Wenar offers the following general formula:

> *Kind-Desire Theory*: Consider a system of norms S that refers to entities under descriptions that are kinds, D and R. If and only if, in circumstances C, a norm of S supports statements of the form:
>
> 1. Some D (qua D) has a duty to *phi* some R (qua R); where "phi" is a verb phrase specifying an action, such as "pays benefit to," "refrain from touching," and "shoot";
> 2. Rs (qua Rs) want such duties to be fulfilled; and
> 3. Enforcement of this duty is appropriate, ceteris paribus;
>
> Then, the R has a claim-right [is owed a duty] in S that the D fulfil this duty in circumstances C. (2013: 219)

Wenar begins from a generic notion of a duty, that is, a requirement on action. Some duties, he says, are owed to others (are directed); others are not. The

---

[70] For compelling counter-examples, see May (2017: 91–4).

[71] For an exception, see Cruft (2017). With Cruft, I've been trying to shift the center of concern to the question of whether reductive analyses of rights succeed.

"mystery is how we know which of these duties is a duty whose performance is owed to some other party" (2013: 208). The general formula of the Kind-Desire model is meant to solve that mystery. Duties are owed to agents in virtue of (i) the fact that a duty exists in a normative system and (ii) agents have kind-based desires that the duty be fulfilled.[72]

For example, Wenar analyzes a parent's right to receive child support as follows. First, there is a self-standing duty in a normative system indicating that the government ought to support children. Second, we note that parents have a kind-based desire to be paid child benefits, "because the money will help them to do their job as parents" (2013: 210). And third, it follows that if the law assigns a duty to government officials to support children, then it also assigns to parents a claim-right to said support, since parents (qua parents) want the officials to pay such child benefits.

Wenar's Kind-Desire theory shares two important features with Interest theory. First, like Interest, the Kind-Desire model aims to offer a reductivist analysis of claim-rights, insofar as Wenar clearly seeks a non-circular explanation. Second, just like Interest seeks to explain the direction of a duty in terms of the interests served by fulfilment of such duties, Wenar seeks to explain the direction of duties in terms of the kind-based desires of an agent.

The contrast between the Kind-Dispositional Model and Wenar's Kind-Desire theory should begin to come into relief.

To begin, both models share a superficial similarity in their emphasis on the kind-based nature of claim-rights. Both theories seek to explain rights in terms of the features of individuals qua members of kinds rather than in terms of features of individuals qua individuals. In addition, I think Wenar is on to something in trying to capture what he calls the enabling function of rights. The Kind-Dispositional model captures such function dispositionally, in terms of the characteristic activities or ways of being of a kind.

Nevertheless, at least four important differences remain.

First, although Wenar appeals to the notions of a social role and of a kind, Wenar never analyzes these notions. By contrast, in the previous section I tried to elucidate the general notion of a kind in terms of the loosely Aristotelian Kind-Dispositional metaphysical framework. And in this section, I connected the Kind-Dispositional model to the Standard Model of Social Ontology, elucidating an important distinction between personal and impersonal social kinds. As we'll see next, once we elucidate the notion of a social role used by Wenar, the account may run into difficulties.

---

[72] I bracket the condition on enforcement.

Second, thinking of practical kinds in terms of the Kind-Dispositional model enabled us to see a conceptual connection between dignity and rights. More precisely, it enabled us to distinguish two fundamental forms of kind-based goodness, Merit-Fixing and Worth-Fixing kinds. By contrast, the Kind-Desire analysis does not set up a conceptual connection between dignity and rights, reinforcing the fairly standard view among philosophers that dignity and rights operate in different conceptual silos.

Third, Wenar's model aims to offer a reductivist analysis of claim-rights. By contrast, the Kind-Dispositional model abandons the model of reductivist analysis in favor of non-reductivist, networked analysis.

But fourth, the Kind-Desire model offers a *specific* kind of reduction. In particular, the model presupposes what, inspired by the work of Margaret Gilbert, we might call a "Duty+" model. The idea is that the analysis takes as basic the notion of an undirected duty, that is, a duty that is not owed to anyone, and then asks what conditions must be *added* in order to get direction. The project, then, is to attempt to reduce the relational notion of a claim-right into the non-relational notion of a duty + some extra ingredients.[73]

However, as Margaret Gilbert argues, there's some reason to be skeptical of the "Duty+" model. The basic idea that correlates with a claim-right is not the notion of some abstract, non-relational duty, out of which non-relational materials the notion of a relational claim is to be constructed. Rather, Gilbert suggests, what is at issue in a theory of claim-rights is that

> A directed obligation is a relation between persons. Owing is clearly a relational matter. One cannot simply "owe" something; one *must* owe it to someone. (2018: 68)

This point matters because it suggests that the notion of owing may not be easily decomposed in terms of a plain duty + direction. Rather, matters may well be the other way around: the notion of relational owing is basic, and the notion of a plain duty is, at best, an abstraction.

Leaning into Gilbert's point helps to elucidate a first challenge for the reductivist structure of the Kind-Desire model. As Rowan Cruft has persuasively argued, we might allow that the Kind-Desire model succeeds in establishing a necessary condition for claim-rights (2019: 23). Yet the approach fails to identify "non-circular sufficient conditions" for claim-rights (2019: 27).

---

[73] A further similarity between Wenar's and Kramer's analysis, I think, is that they are both non-justificatory. That is, unlike Raz, they don't attempt to justify or derive duties, but instead, they take for granted certain duties and then attempt to offer conditions for *identifying* the claim-rights in a normative system. That said, I think an important difference is that Wenar's analysis begins from *undirected duties,* whereas Kramer, following Hohfeld, thinks all duties are directed. If this is correct, it would mean that Kramer's analysis would reject the "duty+" model.

To elaborate the point, Cruft invites you to think through Wenar's own example, a parent's right to child benefit. Recall, the Kind-Desire theory *requires* that if (i) there is an undirected duty by the state with regard to children, and (ii) if parents have a role-based desire in seeing this duty fulfilled, then the normative system puts in place a parent's claim-right to child benefit. On reflection, Cruft argues, the analysis strains. Having a kind-based desire, qua parent, that the state fulfill its duty with regard to child support is not a sufficient condition for parent to possess a claim-right.

> The polity can recognize the existence of this role-based desire, and set up a child benefit system that serves it, without thereby being conceptually compelled to make the duties-to-make-child-benefit-payments duties *owed to parents*. (Cruft 2019: 28)

The key point, as Cruft clarifies, is not that Wenar's model can't explain how the duty is owed to children, but rather the model denies that the duty "could be *unowed* to parents" (2019: 29, fn. 56).

Let me elaborate.[74] Earlier, I argued that a policy of providing for education would satisfy the conditions of a sophisticated conventionalist account without generating rights. We can now see that the same structure applies to Wenar's account. Suppose that there's an imperfect duty of charity to promote the education of the children within a given society. Further, suppose that parents, *qua parents,* have a desire that this policy be implemented, since they have an interest in their children receiving an education. And suppose that, for reasons of efficiency, the policy names parents as recipients of the payments on behalf of the children; that is, parents appear in the content of the duty. These conditions seem to satisfy those of the Kind-Desire model. Yet it's not clear that the education policy would generate a claim-right. Even less clear would it be whether the education policy generates a claim-right possessed by parents. This example, I take it, has the same structure as Cruft's objection.

If so, the objection generalizes. To see this, consider one more example, a policy on housing. Let me stick close to Wenar's formulation.[75] Some *D* (the community as a whole, the government) has a duty to provide housing for *R* (say, the homeless) within the jurisdiction of *D*. Further, the homeless, qua homeless, *want* such duty to be fulfilled, since they would obviously have an interest in accessing housing. Though the two conditions are met, it's not clear that a claim-right has been generated. Why not? The fact that there's a policy to provide housing doesn't entail that the beneficiaries of such policy have a *claim-right* to such service. The reason for this is that the duty in question may be

---

[74] I'm grateful to Wenar for prompting me to elaborate this argument.

[75] I'm grateful to Wenar for pressing me to be more precise in formulating this challenge.

imperfect, say, a duty of charity, or may be owed to the community as a whole – just not to specific homeless individuals.

One way to frame the argument is in terms of *imperfect* duties. First, keep in place the widely held assumption that imperfect duties need not correlate with claim-rights on specific individuals. Now, if we fill in Wenar's conditions, then we get the following result. D (*qua D*) has an imperfect duty with regard to R (*qua R*) (e.g., the community has an imperfect duty of charity to provide for the poor, provide health, housing and education to children); and Rs (*qua R*) may well have a role-based desire that the policy be fulfilled and enforced. Yet, it doesn't seem to follow that Rs, *qua Rs*, have a claim-right to the content of the duty.

The point I'm pressing here is not about extensional correctness, but about explanatory structure. We can bring it out in the form of the following dilemma.[76] On the one hand, if one grants that imperfect duties don't correlate with claim-rights, then it becomes possible to satisfy the conditions of the Kind-Desire model without yielding a claim-right (as I've attempted to illustrate with duties of charity concerning services, such as housing, education, or health). In other words, the analysis doesn't give us *reductive* sufficient conditions for claim-rights. On the other hand, one could deny that the duties in question are *imperfect.* After all, when poverty advocates insist that state provision of health, housing, or education is not a matter of charity but of justice, they're denying that D's duty, *qua D* (e.g., the state qua state) has an imperfect duty. Instead, they insist, the duty of justice is perfect, *correlating with a claim-right.* However, if this is the line taken by the Kind-Desire model, then I grant that it yields *sufficient* conditions for claim-rights – but these will no longer be *non-circular.* Why not? If the duty of justice is perfect, we are supposing, then it's a duty that logically correlates with claim-rights. And if so, the Kind-Desire analysis will work by *presupposing* the very concept it had sought to explain. In short, the dilemma is that if the analysis begins with imperfect, undirected duties, the analysis doesn't yield claim-rights, but if it begins with perfect, directed duties, the analysis yields claim-rights but only by presupposing the notion.

---

[76] I should clarify that in pressing this dilemma, I'm departing from Cruft's line of objection and adding a new one. I'm trying to press the objection more deeply by relying on the distinction between imperfect and perfect duties, which, I believe, Cruft doesn't utilize to elaborate the objection. The reason I do so is that Wenar has objected to me, in correspondence, that the objection can seem to rely barely on the *assertion* that the parents lack claim-rights. This makes it seem as if it's just a matter of intuition whether they have a claim-right. And I think Wenar is right to press this. But once we frame the dilemma in terms of imperfect, undirected duties and perfect, directed ones, I think we have a more robust argument to make the point, one that, hopefully, relies less on the assertion of an intuition. I'm grateful to Wenar for pressing me on this point and, thereby, helping me to sharpen the argument.

Let me elaborate the dilemma by focusing on the second disjunct, the idea that when the Kind-Desire model gives us sufficient conditions, these are not reductive – that is, they involve notions that already make reference to claim-rights.

Start with duties. Wenar's model might seem to have the virtue of reductivist simplicity, but, as I mentioned earlier, the very notion of an undirected duty is contested. For instance, Wenar says that

> the members of the firing squad have a duty to shoot a convict at sunrise, and the convict has no right to be shot. (2013: 207)

The example is supposed to illustrate the notion of an undirected duty: members of the firing squad have a duty to shoot a convict, yet this duty is undirected because there is no correlative right to be shot. But this analysis is misleading, and it does not provide a non-controversial example of an undirected duty. For instance, a Hohfeldian analysis could say that if the members of a firing squad do have duties to shoot a convict, there must be a correlative claim-right. The analysis doesn't tell you *where* to find the correlate, but it tells you *there must be one.* For instance, then, we might analyze the firing squad's duty as owed to their immediate superior or, more generally, to the community as a whole. Matthew Kramer makes the same point, and I think he's exactly right. Kramer argues that Wenar infers from the plausible premise that the convict doesn't have a claim-right to be shot to the conclusion that the duty born by the firing squad is not directed. However, Kramer argues, this is an incorrect inference: the claim-right correlative to that duty is held by the state or by the relevant organ of the state (2017: 73).

The key point, then, is that even if it's a fact that the convict lacks a right to be shot, that doesn't demonstrate the existence of undirected duties. And yet, if the duties in question *are* Hohfeldian, then the theory already presupposes what it sought to explain.

These examples matter because they serve to reinforce the dilemma I articulated previously. If the duties in question really are undirected – perhaps, they are imperfect duties owed to no one in particular – then the Kind-Desire model doesn't give us sufficient conditions to generate claim-rights. On the other hand, if the duties in question are, on reflection, *directed,* then the model yields claim-rights but only by presupposing the notion it had sought to explain. Either way, the reductivist analysis of the Kind-Desire model is in trouble.

Let me elaborate on this dilemma by framing it now in terms of the notion of a *social kind,* the notion, let's suppose, captured by the Standard Model of Social Ontology.

Earlier in this section, I proposed an amendment to the Standard Model of Social Ontology by distinguishing personal from impersonal social kinds, a distinction, say, between a $20 bill and the role of an *operator* under NY DMV.

Now ask: which notion of a social role is operative in the Kind-Desire Model? Not only does the Kind-Desire model treat the notion of an undirected duty as a primitive, it also doesn't explain the notion of a *social kind*. To be sure, the Kind-Desire model may repudiate the Standard Model of Social Ontology altogether. If so, we would be owed an account of what a social role is supposed to be.

But suppose the Kind-Desire model takes on the Standard Model.[77] It seems to me that doing so would replicate the structure of the dilemma I've just articulated.

On the one hand, the Kind-Desire Model could explain social roles in terms of *impersonal social kinds.* On this proposal, all social roles would be reducible to *impersonal social kinds,* like $20 bills or religious symbols. And we can grant, for the sake of argument, that the notion of an impersonal social kind does not require the notion of a claim-right. But if so, it's not clear that the explanation would *guarantee* the presence of a claim-right. If a social role in the Kind-Desire model is no more than an impersonal social kind, then the model can preserve its reductivist ambitions – but it would not explain claim-rights.

It is hard (for me at least) to imagine such a counter-example, but perhaps we could think here of Joel Feinberg's fabled *Nowheresville* (1970). Feinberg's thought experiment is that of a society, *Nowheresville,* where we gradually introduce certain properties and relations – even normative properties and relations – without thereby introducing claim-rights. The point of the thought experiment is to elucidate the notion of a claim-right. Well, let's put Feinberg's *Nowheresville* to use here. Imagine a society constituted exclusively by *impersonal* social kinds, that is, kinds regulated even by undirected duties but without claim-rights at all. Perhaps, we could imagine a system of traffic norms that instantiates this structure, a system with stop signs, green lights, and speed limits. And here, we could add *operators,* individuals who drive within the system. Feinberg's point was that even adding certain normative properties – like simple prohibitions or permissions – is not sufficient to introduce claim-rights. If Feinberg's point is correct, it seems to me, it transposes to the Kind-Desire Theory.

Nowheresville would have social roles that satisfy Kind-Desire conditions. First, we could imagine that the community as a whole (D qua D) has duties

---

[77] In correspondence, Wenar has indicated to me that he'd welcome the Standard Model of Social Ontology as a way to elaborate the notion of a social role. However, as I'm about to argue, opting into this model is a path that may replicate the dilemma I've just articulated.

with regard to operators (*R qua R*). For instance, the community has duties to set up stop signs and speed limits. Second, we could imagine that operators (*R qua R*) *want* these duties to be fulfilled. After all, they appreciate that *qua operators* they have an interest in others following these rules so that they can move around and operate their vehicles in relative safety. But if so, it seems, we have a way of satisfying the conditions of the *Kind-Desire* model through impersonal social kinds without yielding claim-rights on any one, since, Feinberg would insist, this society of operators has undirected duties but no claim-rights.

Alternatively, in order to guarantee the presence of claim-rights, the Kind-Desire Model could coopt the resources of the Standard Model of Social Ontology by analyzing social roles in terms of *personal social kinds*. Here, we'd come closer to Searle and Ludwig's view that the notion of a right in general and the notion of a claim-right in particular is *constitutive of social roles*. The notion of the social kind *operator* is now personal – rather than impersonal, as in Feinberg's *Nowheresville*. And this notion *would suffice* to generate claim-rights, since claim-rights are constitutive of the social role, namely, the personal social kind *operator*. However, the Standard Model analyzes the notion of a social role, say, of a D-Class Driver in terms of status functions, but such status functions *conceptually presuppose* deontic notions like rights. The Standard Model says that the very notion of occupying the social role, *D-Class Driver,* already makes reference to the distinctive claim-rights individuals are assigned in the normative system. But if so, the Kind-Desire model would purchase explanatory power at the cost of abandoning its reductivist ambitions, since the notion of a social role it employs already conceptually contains the notion of a claim-right constitutive of the kind.

This is another example of the general dilemma for reductivist accounts. Earlier, the dilemma was formulated in terms of imperfect and perfect duties. Now, the dilemma depends on the two concepts of social kinds implicit in the Standard Model of Social ontology. In short, this second version of the dilemma is that if the Kind-Desire model uses the model to understand social roles as *impersonal* social kinds, then the model fails to produce *sufficient* conditions for claim-rights. I pressed this disjunct by harnessing the power of Feinberg's celebrated thought-experiment, *Nowheresville.* If the notion of the social kind, *operator,* within a system of traffic norms is impersonal, then it fails to generate claim-rights on anyone. However, if the Kind-Desire model seeks more explanatory power by understanding social roles in terms of *personal social kinds,* then I concede that the model generates *sufficient* conditions for claim-rights – but these will no longer be *non-circular,* since the notion of a personal social kind involves status functions that already make reference to deontic notions like claim-rights.

Is this dilemma fatal to the Kind-Desire Model?[78] I don't know and my point was not to show that it is. Instead, I had two much more modest aims. First, I wanted to clarify the conceptual contrast between the Kind-Desire and the Kind-Dispositional models. The former is reductivist about claim-rights, the latter isn't. Second, I wanted to elaborate a series of arguments exploiting the general structure of the challenge for reductivist accounts, namely, that they either tend not to yield sufficient conditions or, when they do, such conditions are circular. The two key versions of this dilemma turn on the distinction between perfect and imperfect duties and the distinction between personal and impersonal social kinds.

Conclusion

This concludes my argument in this section. I've suggested that the Kind-Dispositional Model offers a distinctive elucidation of the rationale of social rights and the social dimension of dignity. Unlike familiar naturalist and conventionalist views, the Kind-Dispositionalist model understands the role of social kinds as partly constitutive of basic dignity and fundamental rights: social kinds give expression to and fully complete the reality of pre-conventional normative properties.

But to articulate the notion of a social kind, I turned to some of the leading work of metaphysicians and their "Standard Model of Social Ontology." It turns out that not only does the Kind-Dispositional model fit particularly well with the Standard Model, it also can help to elucidate further the notion of a social kind by distinguishing personal from impersonal social kinds. Much more work is needed to continue to develop this synergy between a theory of rights and social ontology. And it may turn out that alternative models fare better than I have argued here. Regardless, my hope is that having opened a more serious investigation into the natural and social metaphysics of dignity and rights, we can continue to move past the familiar impasses generated by reductivist accounts and achieve a greater understanding of two of the most fundamental concepts of our practical self-understanding, our dignity and our rights.

---

[78] I'm particularly grateful to Wenar for his thoughtful and constructive responses to a previous version of this section. They have helped me to sharpen the reductivist dilemma.

References

Alexander, Michelle. 2010. *The New Jim Crow: Mass Incarceration in the Age of Colorblindness*. New York: New Press.

Appiah, Kwame Anthony. 2011. *The Honor Code: How Moral Revolutions Happen*. W. W. Norton.

Armstrong, David, Charlie Martin, and Ullin Place. 1996. *Dispositions: A Debate*. Edited by Tim Crane. London: Routledge.

Beitz, Charles. 2009. *The Idea of Human Rights*. Oxford: Oxford University Press.
2013. "Human Dignity in the Theory of Human Rights: Nothing but a Phrase?" *Philosophy and Public Affairs* 41 (3): 259–90.

Bentham, Jeremy. 1987. "Anarchical Fallacies: Being an Examination of the Declaration of Rights Issued during the French Revolution." In *Nonsense upon Stilts: Bentham, Burke and Marx on the Rights of Man*, edited by Jeremy Waldron, 46–76. New York: Routledge.

Bird, Colin. 2021. *Human Dignity and Political Criticism*. Cambridge: Cambridge University Press.

Christiano, Thomas. 2008. "Two Conceptions of the Dignity of Persons." *Jahrbuch Für Recht Und Ethik / Annual Review of Law and Ethics* 16: 101–26.

Cohon, Rachel. 2006. *Hume's Morality: Feeling and Fabrication*. Oxford: Oxford University Press.

Cornell, Nicholas. 2019. "Review of Rights and Demands: A Foundational Inquiry, by Margaret Gilbert." *Ethics* 130 (January): 107–13.
2015. "Wrongs, Rights, and Third Parties." *Philosophy and Public Affairs* 43 (2): 109–43.

Cruft, Rowan. 2017. "The Circularity of the Interest and Will Theories of Rights." In *New Essays on the Nature of Rights*, edited by Mark McBride, 169–86. Oxford: Hart.
2019. *Human Rights, Ownership, and the Individual*. Oxford: Oxford University Press.

D'Almeida, Luís Duarte. 2016. "Fundamental Legal Concepts: The Hohfeldian Framework." *Philosophy Compass* 11 (10): 554–69.

Darby, Derrick. 2009. *Rights, Race, and Recognition*. Cambridge: Cambridge University Press.

Darwall, Stephen. 1977. "Two Kinds of Respect." *Ethics* 88 (1): 36–49.
2006. *The Second-Person Standpoint : Morality, Respect, and Accountability*. Cambridge, MA: Harvard University Press.

2013. *Morality, Authority, and Law: Essays in Second-Personal Ethics I.* Oxford: Oxford University Press.

2013. *Honor, History, and Relationship: Essays in Second-Personal Ethics II.* Oxford: Oxford University Press.

2017. "Equal Dignity and Rights." In *Dignity: A History*, edited by Remy Debes, 181–202. Oxford: Oxford University Press.

Düwell, Marcus, Jens Braarvig, Roger Brownsword et al. 2015. *The Cambridge Handbook of Human Dignity: Interdisciplinary Perspectives*. Cambridge: Cambridge University Press.

Ebels-Duggan, Kyla. 2012. "Kant's Political Philosophy." *Philosophy Compass* 7 (12): 896–909.

Fabre, Cécile. 2006. *Whose Body Is It Anyway? Justice and the Integrity of the Person*. Oxford: Oxford University Press.

Feinberg, Joel. 1970. "The Nature and Value of Rights." *The Journal of Value Inquiry* 4 (4): 243–60.

Foot, Philippa. 2001. *Natural Goodness*. Oxford: Oxford University Press.

Formosa, Paul. 2017. *Kantian Ethics, Dignity and Perfection*. Cambridge: Cambridge University Press.

Formosa, Paul, and Catriona Mackenzie. 2014. "Nussbaum, Kant, and the Capabilities Approach to Dignity." *Ethical Theory and Moral Practice* 17 (5): 875–92.

Forst, Rainer. 2011. *The Right to Justification: Elements of a Constructivist Theory of Justice*. New York: Columbia University Press.

Gilabert, Pablo. 2015. "Human Rights, Human Dignity, and Power." In *Philosophical Foundations of Human Rights*, edited by Rowan Cruft, Matthew Liao, and Massimo Renzo, 196–214. Oxford: Oxford University Press.

2019. *Human Dignity and Human Rights*. Oxford: Oxford University Press.

Gilbert, Margaret. 2018. *Rights and Demands: A Foundational Inquiry*. Oxford: Oxford University Press.

Green, Leslie. 2010. "Two Worries about Respect for Persons." *Ethics* 120 (2): 212–31.

Griffin, James. 2008. *On Human Rights*. Oxford: Oxford University Press.

Hart, H. L. A. 1955. "Are There Any Natural Rights?" *The Philosophical Review* 64 (2): 175–91.

1982. *Essays on Bentham : Studies in Jurisprudence and Political Theory*. Oxford: Oxford University Press.

Hasan, Rafeeq. 2018. "The Provisionality of Property Rights in Kant's Doctrine of Right." *Canadian Journal of Philosophy* 48 (6): 850–76.

Haslanger, Sally. 2003. "Social Construction: The 'Debunking' Project." In *Socializing Metaphysics*, edited by Frederick Schmitt, 301–25. Oxford: Rowman and Littlefield.

Herman, Barbara. 2021. *The Moral Habitat*. Oxford: Oxford University Press.

Hobbes, Thomas. 1996. *Leviathan: Revised Student Edition*. Edited by Richard Tuck. Cambridge: Cambridge University Press.

Hodgson, Louis Philippe. 2010. "Kant on the Right to Freedom: A Defense." *Ethics* 120 (4): 791–819.

Hohfeld, W. N. 1919. *Fundamental Legal Conceptions as Applied in Judicial Reasoning*. New Haven, CT: Yale University Press.

Irwin, Terence. 2008. *The Development of Ethics: A Historical and Critical Study. Vol. 2, from Suarez to Rousseau*. Oxford: Oxford University Press.

Jackson, Frank, and Philip Pettit. 1995. "Moral Functionalism and Moral Motivation." *The Philosophical Quarterly* 45 (178): 20–40.

Jonker, Julian. 2020. "Directed Duties and Moral Repair." *Philosopher's Imprint* 20 (23): 1–32.

Kagan, Shelly. 1998. *Normative Ethics*. London: Routledge.

Killmister, Suzy. 2017. "Dignity: Personal, Social, Human." *Philosophical Studies* 174 (8): 2063–82.

2020. *Contours of Dignity*. Oxford: Oxford University Press.

Korsgaard, Christine M. 1996. *Creating the Kingdom of Ends*. Cambridge: Cambridge University Press.

Kramer, Matthew. 1998. "Rights without Trimmings." In *A Debate over Rights*, edited by Matthew Kramer, Neil Simmonds, and Hillel Steiner, 7–112. Oxford: Oxford University Press.

2017. "In Defence of the Interest Theory of Right-Holding: Rejoinders to Leif Wenar on Rights." In *New Essays on the Nature of Rights*, edited by Portland, OR: Mark McBride, 49–84. Hart.

Kurki, Visa A. J. 2021. "The Interest Theory of Rights: Still Standing." *Legal Theory* 27 (4): 352–64.

Lowe, Edward J. 1989. *Kinds of Being: A Study of Individuation, Identity and the Logic of Sortal Terms*. Oxford: Blackwell.

Ludwig, Kirk. 2017. *From Plural to Institutional Agency: Collective Action II*. Oxford: Oxford University Press.

Manby, Bronwen. 2016. *Citizenship Law in Africa: A Comparative Study*. New York: Open Society Foundations.

Marmodoro, Anna, ed. 2010. *The Metaphysics of Powers: Their Grounding and Their Manifestations*. New York: Routledge.

Marmodoro, Anna, and Mayr Erasmus. 2019. *Metaphysics: An Introduction to Contemporary Debates and Their History*. Oxford: Oxford University Press.

Martin, Charles B. 2008. *The Mind in Nature*. Oxford: Clarendon Press.

Martin, Rex. 1993. *A System of Rights*. Oxford: Oxford University Press.

May, Simon. 2012. "Moral Status and the Direction of Duties." *Ethics* 113: 113–128.

2017. "Desires, Interests, and Claim-Rights." In *New Essays on the Nature of Rights*, edited by Mark McBride, 85–98. Portland, OR: Hart.

McBride, Mark. 2017. "The Tracking Theory of Rights." In *New Essays on the Nature of Rights*, edited by Mark McBride, 149–68. Oxford: Hart.

2020. "Preserving the Interest Theory of Rights." *Legal Theory* 26 (1): 3–39.

McCrudden, Christopher, ed. 2014. *Understanding Human Dignity: Understanding Human Dignity*. Oxford: Oxford University Press.

Molnar, George. 2003. *Powers: A Study in Metaphysics*. Oxford: Oxford University Press.

Moore, G. E. 1903. *Principia Ethica*. Cambridge: Cambridge University Press.

Mumford, Stephen. 1998. *Dispositions*. Oxford: Oxford University Press.

Nussbaum, Martha. 2008. "Human Dignity and Political Entitlements." In *Human Dignity and Bioethics: Essays Commissioned by the President's Council on Bioethics*, 351–380. President's Council on Bioethics.

2007. *Frontiers of Justice*: Cambridge, MA: Harvard University Press.

Orend, Brian. 2002. *Human Rights: Concept and Context*. Peterborough: Broadview Press.

Owens, David. 2012. *Shaping the Normative Landscape*. Oxford: Oxford University Press.

Pallikkathayil, Japa. 2010. "Deriving Morality from Politics: Rethinking the Formula of Humanity." *Ethics* 121 (1): 116–47.

2017. "Persons and Bodies." In *Freedom and Force: Essays on Kant's Legal Philosophy*, edited by Sari Kisilevsky and Martin Jay Stone, 35–54. Portland, OR: Bloomsbury.

Pinker, Stephen. 2008. "The Stupidity of Dignity." *The New Republic*. https://newrepublic.com/article/64674/the-stupidity-dignity.

Pippin, Robert B. 2006. "Mine and Thine? The Kantian State." In *The Cambridge Companion to Kant and Modern Philosophy*, edited by Paul Guyer, 416–46. Cambridge, MA: Cambridge University Press.

Rainbolt, George W. 2006. *The Concept of Rights*. Dordrecht: Springer.

Raz, Joseph. 1986. *The Morality of Freedom*. Oxford: Clarendon Press.

Reale, Miguel. 2004. "Values and the Realm of Ought to Be." In *Latin American Philosophy for the 21st Century*, 205–14. Lanham, MD: National Book Network.

Rescher, Nicholas. 2000. *Process Philosophy: A Survey of Basic Issues*. Pittsburgh, PA: University of Pittsburgh Press.

Ripstein, Arthur. 2009. *Force and Freedom: Kant's Legal and Political Philosophy*. Cambridge, MA: Harvard University Press.

Rosen, Michael. 2012. *Dignity: Its History and Meaning*. Cambridge, MA: Harvard University Press.

2013. "Dignity: The Case against." In *Understanding Human Dignity*, edited by Christopher McCrudden, 143–54. Oxford: Oxford University Press.

Ryle, Gilbert. 2009. *The Concept of Mind*. Oxford: Routledge.

Sangiovanni, Andrea. 2017. *Humanity without Dignity: Moral Equality, Respect, and Human Rights*. Cambridge, MA: Harvard University Press.

Schaab, Janis David. 2023. "Second-Personal Approaches to Moral Obligation." *Philosophy Compass* 18 (3): 1–11.

Schneewind, Jerome B. 1997. *The Invention of Autonomy: A History of Modern Moral Philosophy*. Cambridge: Cambridge University Press.

Searle, John R. 2010. *Making the Social World: The Structure of Human Civilization*. Oxford: Oxford University Press.

Setiya, Kieran. 2022. "What Is Morality?" *Philosophical Studies* 179 (4): 1113–33.

Shafer-Landau, Russ. 2003. *Moral Realism: A Defence*. Oxford: Oxford University Press.

Simmons, A. John. 1992. *The Lockean Theory of Rights*. Princeton, NJ: Princeton University Press.

Skorupski, John. 2010. *The Domain of Reasons*. Oxford: Oxford University Press.

Sreenivasan, Gopal. 2005. "A Hybrid Theory of Claim-Rights." *Oxford Journal of Legal Studies* 25 (2): 257–74.

2017. "Public Goods, Individual Rights and Third-Party Benefits." In *New Essays on the Nature of Rights*, edited by Mark McBride, 127–48. Portland, OR: Hart.

Steiner, Hillel. 1994. *An Essay on Rights*. Cambridge, MA: Blackwell.

2002. "Working Rights." In *A Debate over Rights: Philosophical Inquiries*, edited by Simmonds Kramer, and Steiner, 233–302. Oxford: Oxford University Press.

Stone, Martin Jay, and Rafeeq Hasan. 2022. "What Is Provisional Right?" *The Philosophical Review* 131 (1): 51–98.

Strassera, Julio. 2024. "'Nunca Más: Alegato Del Fiscal Julio Strassera'." www .Elhistoriador.Com.Ar/Nunca-Mas-Alegato-Del-Fiscal-Julio-Cesar-Strassera/.

Strawson, Peter F. 1992. *Analysis and Metaphysics: An Introduction to Philosophy*. Oxford: Oxford University Press.

Tasioulas, John. 2013. "Human Dignity and the Foundations of Human Rights." In *Understanding Dignity*, edited by Christopher McCrudden, 291–312. Oxford: Oxford University Press.

Thompson, Michael. 2004. "What Is It to Wrong Someone? A Puzzle about Justice." In *Reason and Value: Themes from the Moral Philosophy of Joseph Raz*, edited by R. Jay Wallace, Philip Pettit, Samuel Scheffler, and Michael Smith, 333–84. Oxford: Oxford University Press.

2008. *Life and Action: Elementary Structures of Practice and Practical Thought*. Cambridge, MA: Harvard University Press.

Thomson, Judith Jarvis. 1992. *The Realm of Rights*. Cambridge, MA: Harvard University Press.

2008. *Normativity*. Chicago, IL: Open Court.

Tuck, Richard. 1979. *Natural Rights Theories: Their Origin and Development*. Cambridge: Cambridge University Press.

1999. *The Rights of War and Peace : Political Thought and the International Order from Grotius to Kant*. New York: Oxford University Press.

Vandieken, Jonas. 2019. "Bipolar Obligations, Recognition Respect, and Second-Personal Morality." *Journal of Ethics* 23 (3): 291–315.

Vlastos, Gregory. 1984. "Justice and Equality." In *Theories of Rights*, edited by Jeremy Waldron, 41–76. Oxford: Oxford University Press.

Waldron, Jeremy. 1993. *Liberal Rights: Collected Papers, 1981–1991*. Cambridge: Cambridge University Press.

2012. *Dignity, Rank, and Rights*. Edited by Meir Dan-Cohen. Oxford: Oxford University Press.

Wallace, R. Jay. 2013. "The Deontic Structure of Morality." In *Thinking about Reasons: Themes from the Philosophy of Jonathan Dancy*, edited by David Bakhurst, Brad Hooker, and Margaret Olivia Little, 137–67. Oxford: Oxford University Press.

2019. *The Moral Nexus*. Princeton: Princeton University Press.

Wedgwood, Ralph. 2007. *The Nature of Normativity*. Oxford: Oxford University Press.

Wenar, Leif. 2013. "The Nature of Claim-Rights." *Ethics* 123 (2): 321–43.

Wood, Allen W. 1999. *Kant's Ethical Thought*. Cambridge: Cambridge University Press.

Zylberman, Ariel. 2016. Human Dignity. *Philosophy Compass*. 11 (4), 201–210.

2018. "The Relational Structure of Human Dignity." *Australasian Journal of Philosophy* 96 (4): 738–52.

2022. "Review of Colin Bird, Human Dignity and Political Criticism." *Notre Dame Philosophical Reviews*. https://ndpr.nd.edu/.

2023b. "The Relational Wrong of Poverty." Ethical Theory and Moral Practice 26 (2): 303–19.

2025. "Rights and the Good." The Philosophical Quarterly 75 (1): 288–309.

Acknowledgments

I first began thinking seriously about dignity and rights while working for the Peruvian Human Rights NGO, APRODEH, as a witness to the fight for justice among the Indigenous Peoples of the Peruvian Andes. Ever since, I've been trying to render philosophically intelligible an idea at the core of fights for justice everywhere.

This particular project began at the invitation of George Pavlakos, series editor for the Cambridge Elements in the Philosophy of Law. George's support, wise guidance, and encouragement literally made this Element possible. Thank you, George.

I began writing this Element a few years ago at my home institution, University at Albany, SUNY. My incredibly supportive and collegial colleagues have provided me with an ideal environment in which to do philosophy. In particular, thanks to Brad Armour-Garb, Rachel Cohon, Jason D'Cruz, Kristen Hessler, and Jon Mandle for stimulating conversations on the Element's topic. Jon, in particular, read the entire manuscript and provided invaluable feedback. My department also enabled me to teach a seminar on the topic of this Element, which greatly helped in my writing. I'd like to thank the graduate students who participated in that seminar for help and a lively intellectual community in which to test out ideas. Thanks to Nick Boles, Bailey Cordell, Jenn Eby, Jonah Ford, Marla Hasin, Joel Kapapa, Caelan Knapp, Kei Yan Leun, Connor Menneto, and Rudy Stegemoeller. In this seminar I was fortunate to count on the guest participation of terrific colleagues from the philosophical community: Steve Darwall, Giacomo Floris, Pablo Gilabert, Margaret Gilbert, and Kieran Setiya. In addition to personal illumination, I invited these philosophers to participate in my seminar in order to convey to my students the sense that philosophy is not a dead set of doctrines to be learned, but a living, breathing, and collaborative intellectual community. I consider myself extremely fortunate to be part of such a community.

I'm particularly grateful to the following members of such a community for help, conversation, and encouragement with this project: Monika Betzler, G. Anthony Bruno, Brendan de Kenessey, Tom Christiano, Nico Cornell, Steve Darwall, Pablo Gilabert, Micha Gläser, Tom Hurka, Rafeeq Hasan, Barbara Herman, Chris Howard, Eliot Michaelson, Karin Nisenbaum, Arthur Ripstein, Oliver Sensen, Andrew Sepielli, Dave Suarez, Laura Valentini, Jonas Vandieken, R. Jay Wallace, Jordan Walters, Owen Ware, and Daniel Weinstock. I'm particularly grateful to Rowan Cruft, Suzy Killmister, Leif Wenar, and

Jacob Weinrib for providing detailed, probing, and constructive feedback on the entire manuscript. Two anonymous referees for the press shared detailed and thoughtful feedback that saved me from many errors and helped me clarify further key ideas.

If debts are quantifiable, then the greatest debt of gratitude I owe to my family. My parents, Marta and Mauricio, never once questioned my project to pursue philosophy and supported me unconditionally. But making philosophy work proved far more personally trying than I would have envisaged. The unconditional support, love, and understanding I received from Claire, Zoe (who also provided invaluable research assistance), Noah, and Hugo not only made this particular project possible; it also made my career in philosophy a reality. I dedicate this work to them.

Cambridge Elements ⹀

Philosophy of Law

Series Editors

George Pavlakos
University of Glasgow

George Pavlakos is Professor of Law and Philosophy at the School of Law, University of Glasgow. He has held visiting posts at the universities of Kiel and Luzern, the European University Institute, the UCLA Law School, the Cornell Law School and the Beihang Law School in Beijing. He is the author of *Our Knowledge of the Law* (2007) and more recently has co-edited *Agency, Negligence and Responsibility* (2021) and *Reasons and Intentions in Law and Practical Agency* (2015).

Gerald J. Postema
University of North Carolina at Chapel Hill

Gerald J. Postema is Professor Emeritus of Philosophy at the University of North Carolina at Chapel Hill. Among his publications count *Utility, Publicity, and Law: Bentham's Moral and Legal Philosophy* (2019); *On the Law of Nature, Reason, and the Common Law: Selected Jurisprudential Writings of Sir Matthew Hale* (2017); *Legal Philosophy in the Twentieth Century: The Common Law World* (2011), *Bentham and the Common Law Tradition*, 2nd edition (2019).

Kenneth M. Ehrenberg
University of Surrey

Kenneth M. Ehrenberg is Professor of Jurisprudence and Philosophy at the University of Surrey School of Law and Co-Director of the Surrey Centre for Law and Philosophy. He is the author of *The Functions of Law* (2016) and numerous articles on the nature of law, jurisprudential methodology, the relation of law to morality, practical authority, and the epistemology of evidence law.

Associate Editor

Sally Zhu
University of Sheffield

Sally Zhu is a Lecturer in Property Law at University of Sheffield. Her research is on property and private law aspects of platform and digital economies.

About the Series

This series provides an accessible overview of the philosophy of law, drawing on its varied intellectual traditions in order to showcase the interdisciplinary dimensions of jurisprudential enquiry, review the state of the art in the field, and suggest fresh research agendas for the future. Focussing on issues rather than traditions or authors, each contribution seeks to deepen our understanding of the foundations of the law, ultimately with a view to offering practical insights into some of the major challenges of our age.

Cambridge Elements $\equiv$

Philosophy of Law

Elements in the Series

Hans Kelsen's Normativism
Carsten Heidemann

The Materiality of the Legal Order
Marco Goldoni

Sociological Approaches to Theories of Law
Brian Z. Tamanaha

Revisiting the Rule of Law
Kristen Rundle

The Place of Coercion in Law
Triantafyllos Gkouvas

The Differentiation and Autonomy of Law
Emilios Christodoulidis

*The Moral Prerequisites of the Criminal Law: Legal Moralism
and the Problem of* Mala Prohibita
Ambrose Y. K. Lee and Alexander F. Sarch

Legal Personhood
Visa A. J. Kurki

The Philosophy of Legal Proof
Lewis Ross

The Normativity of Law
Michael Giudice

Legal Rights and Moral Rights
Matthew H. Kramer

Dignity and Rights
Ariel Zylberman

A full series listing is available at: www.cambridge.org/EPHL

Printed in the United States
by Baker & Taylor Publisher Services